GLOBAL
HISTORY & GEOGRAPHY
REGENTS REVIEW

Designed for the New 2019 Exam Format

Joan Medori, B.A., M.A.
Joseph Cocurullo, B.A.

Teach 'n
Thrive

teachandthrive@gmail·com

For free teaching resources, such as slide presentations, exams, reading passages, and how-to articles visit my website at Teachnthrive.com

Table of Contents

Constructed Response Questions Explained (CRQ)

The historian skills necessary to understand and complete this part of the exam include:
Contextualization AND Sourcing AND Causation

QUESTION 1
You will be asked to explain EITHER the historical circumstances OR geographic circumstances.
This means you need to explain the CAUSE, what happened leading up to the event shown in the document.
Example: Before this political cartoon, most products were made by hand at home or in small shops.

QUESTION 3
YOU _MUST_ INCLUDE BOTH DOCUMENTS IN YOUR ANSWER
You will be asked 1 of the following:
Cause and Effect: How 1 source led to the other
OR
Turning Point: Identify the big change AND explain how each document led to the change
OR
Comparison: Explain a similarity or difference between the 2 sources.

QUESTION 2
You will be asked to explain EITHER the
Point of view; author's opinion
Example: The author of this cartoon is in favor of capitalism
OR
Bias; whether a source is neutral or not
Example: The author of this cartoon shows only the benefits of capitalism without addressing the negative effects.
OR
Audience: who the source is created for
Example: The intended audience of this cartoon are British citizens during the Industrial Revolution
OR
Purpose: why the source was created
Example: The purpose of this political cartoon was to encourage citizens to support capitalism.

You got this!

Enduring Issues Essay

Definition; An enduring issue is a challenge or problem that a society has faced and debated or discussed across time. It is a topic that many societies have attempted to address with varying degrees of success.

An enduring issue can big a big issue, like conflict, or a sub-issue like ethnic disputes. Your enduring issue can be any big issue or sub-issue, if you can justify it with evidence from the documents (SUPER important!)

It is **crucial that you choose only 1 enduring issue** to write your essay about. Here's how to find the enduring issue:
1. After studying each document write down the issues covered in it
2. Find a common category that is addressed in at least 3 of the documents.
3. That category is your enduring issue!

Example: 1 document is about tensions between 2 places because of water supply, another document covers food insecurity, a third is about desertification, the 4th document describing OPEC's influence in the world.

An enduring issue that you might have chosen is scarcity. Another student may choose to write about human impact on the environment. You're BOTH right!

Examples of Enduring Issues

 You DON'T have to memorize these enduring issues and there are MANY more possibilities. This is a guide.

Enduring Issue	Subtopics of the Issue
Human Rights Violation	Genocide, discrimination, unequal treatment, enslavement, human trafficking
Human Impact on the Environment	deforestation, desertification, global warming, pollution, extinction of species/loss of Species, land-use disputes
Population increase	Strain on resources, ability to feed the population, social services
Conflict	War, disputes over boundaries, disputes over land, response to lack of reform
Impact of cultural diffusion	Debate over values, threat to cultural identify, spread of ideas
Impact of technology	Impact of technology on people, on the environment, on economies, on settling conflicts
Scarcity	Lack of food, natural resources, housing, medical treatment
Impact of Imperialism	Challenge of controlling land, challenge of colonization, maintaining control of territory, challenge of exerting power, ability to supply people living in controlled territories
Impact of Trade	introduction of new goods, distribution and access to new goods, loss of traditional beliefs, impact on raising standards of living, impact of changes in production
Desire for Power	Lack of access to power, shifts in the balance of power, access to free and fair elections, lack of free and fair elections

Did you notice that many of the enduring issues are about the "impact" of something? Impact refers to the effects a change has on society.

Identifying Your Enduring Issues

1. Study each document and write down the issues covered
2. Find a common category that is addressed in at least 3 of the documents.
3. That category is your enduring issue!

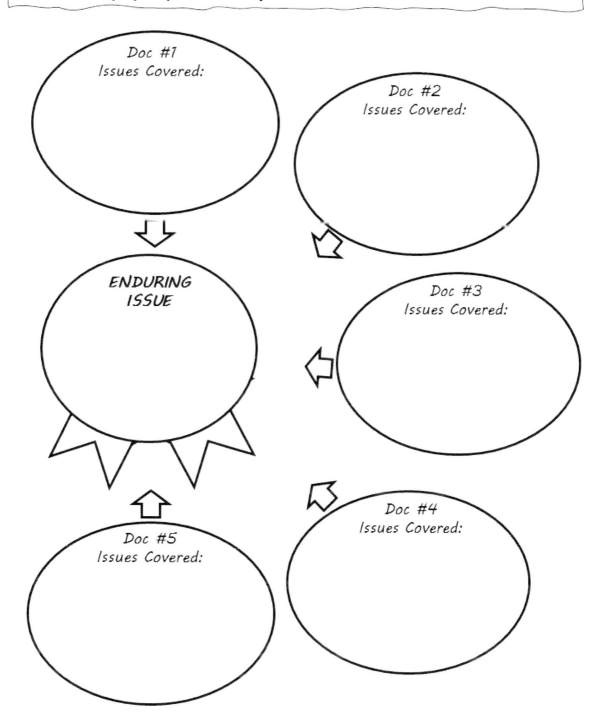

Name _____ Date _____

Enduring Issues Essay Outline

Enduring Issue Chosen:
_____

Definition/Description: (this goes in your intro)

Doc. #	Evidence of Enduring Issue	Explanation
1st body para		
2nd body para		
3rd body para		

Conclusion: Why is this enduring issue significant (important)?

Scientific Revolution

The Renaissance included changes in scientific thought, generally seen as beginning in the mid-16th Century (1500's). Long-held scientific understandings based on Ancient Greek and Roman learning and teachings of the church were questioned. This provided a path to modern scientific thought and all that came from it.

Scientific Method

The scientific method is a method of obtaining knowledge, advanced by the scientist **Francis Bacon**. It is based on observation and experimentation to prove a theory is correct. The scientific method often provided a more open mind, doubting even well-accepted beliefs that existed without proof and providing independent evidence of new ideas.

An alternative approach was furthered by people such as the French scientist **René Descartes**, who used reason to develop scientific knowledge. For instance, he hypothesized that fundamentally he existed because he was able to reason ("I think, therefore I am"). Science developed as a mix of both approaches, including the development of theoretical mathematics as well as more experiential methods (based on observation).

Astronomy

Astronomy is the study of celestial objects such as stars, while astrology is the belief such objects could help explain human affairs. Astronomy had ancient roots and had practical uses, such as for navigation of ships. Inventions such as the sextant, a device to determine the distance between two objects, helped promote the Age of Exploration. It also helps explain how the universe itself works.

The traditional view was that the earth was the center of the solar system (**geocentric view**), which seemed to be true by observation and matched biblical texts. In the 16th Century, the astronomer **Nicolaus Copernicus**, helped with the discovery of the telescope that allowed for a more accurate study of the skies.

Before the Scientific Revolution people believed in a **geocentric model** of the universe. This was taught by ancient scientists as well as the Catholic Church. A new understanding was developed that used a **heliocentric** (sun centered) view of the solar system. Further discoveries by such scientists as **Johannes Kepler** and **Galileo** expanded on his work. Galileo was put on trial as a heretic for speaking out against the church's teachings that the universe revolved around the earth. At trial he faced the difficult decision to testify his true beliefs and be executed or back down. He chose life, and on the witness stand retracted his earlier statements that the sun was at the center of the universe.

Isaac Newton, an English scientist, formulated basic **laws of motion and gravity**. He is supposed to have created the theory of gravity after sitting under a tree and having an apple fall on his head. This led him to believe that all things made of matter will fall – whatever goes up, must come down. It also caused him to dislike apples.

Other Developments

Discoveries in astronomy were matched by those in biology and medicine, the technology that provided the telescope also gave us the microscope. This allowed a magnified view of the human body, down to the individual cells, and helped to better understand human anatomy. William Harvey is an example; he studied the circulation of the blood. Developments in chemistry started science on the road to modern understanding of atoms and chemical reactions.

The Scientific Revolution included inventions in a range of fields, such as the development of the first mechanical clocks. The new ways of looking at science also was applied in other ways, influencing political thought. Political thinkers such as **John Locke** used scientific reasoning to explain human behavior and new ways to govern. Ideas taken from the Scientific Revolution were expanded out to many other areas, such as government, society and economics. Thus, the era had diverse significance, helping pave the way to the 18th Century and beyond.

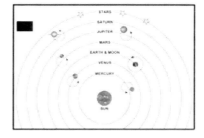

Diagram A   **Diagram B**

1. Diagram A represents
①. the Church's view of the solar system
2. A geometric model of the solar system
3. A heliocentric model of the solar system
4. The sun's position to earth

2. Copernicus' study of the solar system led to his belief
1. that Diagram A was the correct model
②. that Diagram B was the correct model
3. that both Diagram A and B were correct, depending on the season
4. that the gravitational pull of the sun changed its position

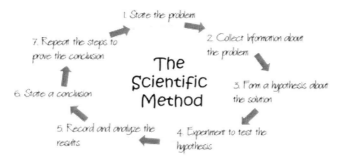

3. The scientist that introduced this formal model of experimentation was
1. Johannes Kepler
2. Nicolaus Copernicus
3. Isaac Newton
4. Francis Bacon

4. Prior to the scientific method science was based on
1. Greek learning and teachings of the Church
2. observation and experimentation
3. the use of microscopes
4. conjecture

5. Step 7, repeat the previous steps, was important
1. to ensure that the conclusion was valid
2. to avoid human error
3. to avoid jumping to conclusions with enough data
4. all the above

> ## Recantation (withdrawing of testimony) of Galileo at his trial (1633)
> *... after an injunction (order to stop) had been judicially intimated to me by this Holy Office, to the effect that I must altogether abandon the false opinion that the sun is the center of the world and immovable, and that the earth is not the center of the world, and moves, and that I must not hold, defend, or teach in any way whatsoever, verbally or in writing, the said false doctrine, and after it had been notified to me that the said doctrine was contrary to Holy Scripture ...*

6. What is the historical circumstances of the document above?
1. Galileo was put on trial for copying Copernicus' telescope
2. The Catholic Church put Galileo on trial for heresy
3. The Holy Office was questioning Galileo's laws of gravity
4. Galileo was teaching contrary to the scientific method

7. What is the purpose of Galileo's testimony in his recantation?
1. to defend his findings on a heliocentric universe
2. to explain his teachings to the Catholic church
3. to change his original testimony in order to avoid execution.
4. to assure the Holy Office that he would not teach anymore

8. Based on the document above, which of the following is a true statement?
1. The Church forbade Galileo to speak, teach or write about a heliocentric universe
2. Galileo promised the Church to teach that the sun is the center of the world
3. The Church was accepting of opinions that differed from theirs
4. The injunction placed on Galileo was contrary to Holy Scripture

> # "If I have seen further it is by standing on the shoulder of giants." - Isaac Newton

9. What is Newton's point of view in this quote?
1. he was short but had tall friends
2. his findings were accepted by the Catholic Church
3. he could see further thanks to a better telescope
4. his scientific discoveries were built from ideas of those before him

10. Which of the following discoveries is attributed to Isaac Newton?
1. the invention of the telescope
2. the theory of relativity
3. laws of motion and gravity
4. all the above

> ### Recantation (withdrawing of testimony) of Galileo at his trial (1633)
> ... after an injunction (order to stop) had been judicially intimated to me by this Holy Office, to the effect that I must altogether abandon the false opinion that the sun is the center of the world and immovable, and that the earth is not the center of the world, and moves, and that I must not hold, defend, or teach in any way whatsoever, verbally or in writing, the said false doctrine, and after it had been notified to me that the said doctrine was contrary to Holy Scripture ...

6. What is the historical circumstances of the document above?
1. Galileo was put on trial for copying Copernicus' telescope
2. The Catholic Church put Galileo on trial for heresy
3. The Holy Office was questioning Galileo's laws of gravity
4. Galileo was teaching contrary to the scientific method

7. What is the purpose of Galileo's testimony in his recantation?
1. to defend his findings on a heliocentric universe
2. to explain his teachings to the Catholic church
3. to change his original testimony in order to avoid execution.
4. to assure the Holy Office that he would not teach anymore

8. Based on the document above, which of the following is a true statement?
1. The Church forbade Galileo to speak, teach or write about a heliocentric universe
2. Galileo promised the Church to teach that the sun is the center of the world
3. The Church was accepting of opinions that differed from theirs
4. The injunction placed on Galileo was contrary to Holy Scripture

> ## "If I have seen further it is by standing on the shoulder of giants." - Isaac Newton

9. What is Newton's point of view in this quote?
1. he was short but had tall friends
2. his findings were accepted by the Catholic Church
3. he could see further thanks to a better telescope
4. his scientific discoveries were built from ideas of those before him

10. Which of the following discoveries is attributed to Isaac Newton?
1. the invention of the telescope
2. the theory of relativity
3. laws of motion and gravity
4. all the above

The Enlightenment

Ignorance can be described as "being in the dark" about something. Likewise, "enlightenment" is finding knowledge, fighting ignorance. Thus, the Enlightenment Era (or the Age of Reason) was an intellectual movement of European history in the 17th and 18th Centuries emphasizing reason and human development.

Philosophy

Philosophy is the study of human knowledge by use of reason while philosophers are those who study philosophy. The use of reason could also be applied to many areas such as science, government and social issues. "Philosophes" was the name of intellectuals of the 18th Century who applied reason to diverse fields.

During this period, human reason, as compared to reliance on religion or tradition, was seen by many as a basic way to handle human affairs. This was a development that arose from such things as the growth of **humanism** (focusing on human thoughts and needs), developments in science (scientific revolution) and religion (Protestant Revolution).

Political Philosophy

Reason was applied to formulate how best to govern with many political philosophers in this era in particular influencing the founding of the United States. Thomas Hobbes was a British philosopher; he wrote Leviathan to discuss his views of the basis of political society. Another influential British political philosopher, particularly in the United States, was **John Locke**. He wrote *Two Treatises of Government* which explained that civilized men give up the total freedom that exists in nature by creating a government that protects its citizens in exchange for following the laws. And, the French philosopher **Montesquieu** (*Spirit of the Laws*) discussed the concept of separation of powers.

A basic concern for all was the concept of a "social contract," a theory describing the justification of governmental or social power over individuals. The French philosopher **Rousseau** also discussed this concept, including in crafting means to educate children. Political philosophy argued government must protect the needs of the people, including limits on government to prevent harm.

Religious Liberty

Enlightenment thought spoke of a "natural law" that not only was a scientific explanation of nature but of human existence as well. It could be discovered by use of reason, which for some left a limited role for a deity (god). Some believed in deism, that God created the universe and basically let it run without interference. If not deists, many still relied largely on rationalism, use of reason as the prime source of knowledge.

Religious Liberty

Enlightenment thought spoke of a "natural law" that not only was a scientific explanation of nature but of human existence as well. It could be discovered by use of reason, which for some left a limited role for a deity (god). Some believed in deism, that God created the universe and basically let it run without interference. If not deists, many still relied largely on rationalism, use of reason as the prime source of knowledge.

There also grew an understanding that church and state should be separate, the "secular state" and religious life separate spheres. Religious institutions, critiqued along with others by such people like **Voltaire** (writer of *Candide*, satirizing European society), must have limits too. Individual religious liberty was key.

Other Areas

As interest grew in exploring new types of governments other areas of study joined in the philosophical contemplation. For instance, **Adam Smith** wrote *The Wealth of Nations*, discussing his economic philosophy such as the promotion of free trade. **Cesare Beccaria**, an Italian philosopher, wrote *On Crime and Punishments* to discuss his views. His writings influenced the Eighth Amendment of the United States Constitution, which bars cruel and unusual punishments.

The **Age of Reason** had wide influence. Enlightenment ideas of natural rights helped lead to revolutions in America, France and Latin America. The ideologies are a cornerstone for the U.S. Constitution.

A pushback to enlightenment ideas ultimately developed known as "romanticism," more focused on emotional life and passions. This flowed into the 19th Century.

> **"If the legislative and executive authorities are one institution, there will be no freedom. There won't be freedom anyway if the judiciary body is not separated from the legislative and executive authorities."**

1. Which enlightenment thinker is quoted above?
1. Thomas Hobbes
2. John Locke
3. Voltaire
4. Baron de Montesquieu

2. What type of government is being suggested?
1. Representative democracy
2. Monarchy
3. Oligarchy
4. Communist

3. Which statement bests describes the message of the quote?
1. that the legislative and executive authorities should be one branch of government
2. that a separation of powers of the government is necessary for freedom
3. the judiciary body should have precedence over the executive and legislative branches
4. it is unnecessary to have all three branches of government

---

Second Treatise of Government – John Locke

THE natural liberty of man is to be free from any superior power on earth, and not to be under the will or legislative authority of man, but to have only the law of nature for his rule. The liberty of man, in society, is to be under no other legislative power, but that established, by consent, in the commonwealth … freedom of men under government is, to have a standing rule to live by, common to every one of that society, and made by the legislative power erected in it; a liberty to follow my own will in all things, where the rule prescribes not; and not to be subject to the inconstant, uncertain, unknown, arbitrary will of another man: as freedom of nature is, to be under no other restraint but the law of nature…

---

4. According to John Locke what is the natural state of man?
1. to be under the authority of a legislative body
2. is to live in society under monarchal rule
3. to create a separation of powers
4. to live under the laws of nature

5. The *Second Treatise of Government* states that man should only follow laws
1. that are written by a government created by consent of the people
2. that ensure every man, woman and child is equal
3. that monarchs must follow as well
4. he should not follow any laws but his own

Adam Smith is considered one of the most influential thinkers of the Enlightenment. He studied moral philosophy at Oxford and conceived of an economic philosophy of "the obvious and simple system of natural liberty," which the world would come to know as capitalism. Following is an excerpt from his book, *The Wealth of Nations*

As every individual, therefore, endeavors as much as he can both to employ his capital in the support of domestic industry, and so to direct that industry that its produce may be of the greatest value; every individual necessarily labors to render the annual revenue of the society as great as he can. He generally, indeed, neither intends to promote the public interest, nor knows how much he is promoting it. . .

6. According the Adam Smith what is the goal of every person?
1. to labor as little as possible
2. to invest his money in order to get the greatest reward possible
3. to promote public interest whenever possible
4. to save the greatest amount of his income as possible

7. How is the idea of capitalism similar to Enlightenment ideas about government?
1. both try to enable everyone to have freedom of religion
2. capitalism would not be possible without a monarchy
3. both ideas stress the importance of natural rights in government and business
4. the 3 branches of government would make economic policy

8. According to *The Wealth of Nations* what is the effect of capitalism?
1. it increases the wealth of all men
2. it helps to promote the public good naturally
3. capitalism will lead to a democratic government
4. entrepreneurs will create products even if the public does not need it

9. What are the historical circumstances of this political cartoon?
1. Enlightenment ideas of men following laws in exchange for safety
2. the agreement between Napoleon and King George III
3. the publishing of the Declarations of the Rights of Man
4. an Enlightenment Era contract between monarchs and their citizens

10. The Social Contract was an alternative to
1. the loose affiliations of citizens in society
2. the antisocial contract
3. the English Bill of Rights
4. the freedom of man in a natural state

The French Revolution

King Louis XVI of France was a young monarch when his country allied with the American revolutionaries in the United States. It was part of an extended rivalry between England and France, but it would have unexpected consequences at home.

Causes

The costs of the French involvement in the American Revolution, excess spending by the French king, combined with long-time economic problems had devastating effects. The needs of the peasants, including basic ability to have enough food, was seen as not being properly taken care of by a wasteful aristocracy. King Louis XVI and his wife Marie Antoinette at the royal court in **Versailles** were seen as privileged elites, only caring about themselves.

Bread riots, strikes and looting showed the desperation of the people. There was a growing demand for reforms that provided a more equitable system of governmental regulation. This was also influenced by Enlightenment ideas of natural rights, division of power in government and free speech. The American Revolution, just a few years earlier inspired the French citizens. After all, if the colonists could win independence from the powerful British, why couldn't France abolish their monarchy?

The Estate System

France was at this time divided into three social groups (estates): **the first estate** (church), **second estate** (nobles) and **third estate** (everyone else)

The king in 1789, for the first time in centuries, called together a meeting of representatives of the estates, the **Estates General**, to discuss possible reforms. The Third Estate, the largest group, united together into the "**National Assembly**" to demand reforms. This was formally stated in the **Tennis Court Oath**, demanding constitutional reforms. A new constitution and **Declaration of Rights of Man** were passed, inspired by Enlightenment principles.

Reign of Terror

The great changes to French society, as seen by the establishment of the "First Republic" (1792) to replace a monarchial version (king led) of government with a republican one (government of the people), had less orderly and violent aspects.

The start of the French Revolution is often dated on July 14, 1789 (Bastille Day), involving the **storming of the Bastille**, a prison holding political prisoners. Protests often led to violence, including killing anyone accused of sympathizing with the king.

The king and queen themselves were eventually executed for treason. This began a period of violence and crushing of opponents (1793-4) known as the Reign of Terror. The government was controlled by a group known as the **Jacobins** with a **Committee of Public Safety** to enforce its policies. Thousands were executed by guillotine, an execution device of the time that decapitated its victims.

Napoleon

France also began a growing military conflict with other European powers during this period.

The conflict helped to spread French revolutionary ideas of society and government across Europe, including promoting a more secular (non-religious) approach in a once firmly Catholic nation. Slavery was abolished and the rights of women were also promoted. These changes outlasted the French Revolution itself.

After the Reign of Terror died down, a more moderate government (the Directory) formed. In 1799 **Napoleon**, a French general returned from Egypt and led his armies in a coup d'état, a military overthrow of the French government. He quickly named himself emperor of France, ending the republic which had been established during the revolution. He made reforms to bring peace and stability after the Reign of Terror had devasted France.

After bringing law and order back to France Napoleon set out to expand his empire. By 1812 he controlled most of Europe and replaced the sitting monarchs with friends and relatives.

These conquered nations resented French rule. Citizens rebelled against paying taxes to France and sending their sons to fight in Napoleonic wars. Feelings of **nationalism** – pride in one's country – further weakened France's control over its European conquests.

Another factor that led to Napoleon's downfall was his invasion of Russia. As he attacked from the west Russian troops retreated toward the east. As they left a policy of "**scorched earth**" was implemented. Russian troops would burn the towns and villages as they retreated. This left the incoming French troops without food or shelter. Russia's brutal winter killed most of Napoleon's troops. In March of 1814 Napoleon was defeated. He was exiled (imprisoned) on a remote island where he lived out his days. A brother of King Louis XVI was placed on the throne to rule France.

Congress of Vienna

After the fall of Napoleon European powers gathered in Vienna. The purpose for the conference was to restructure peace in Europe and bring a balance of power to the continent.

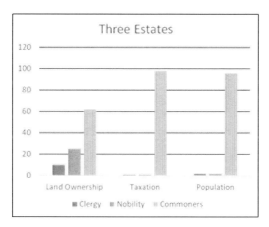

1. Based on the chart above 2 causes of the French Revolution were
1. The French monarch owned most of the land and paid no taxes
2. The Third Estate (commoners) paid most of the taxes and owned too little land
3. the population had increased and the amount of land did not
4. the clergy did not pay their share of taxes and the nobles paid too much

2. Prior to the French Revolution
1. a commoner could become a noble through land ownership
2. King Louis XIV treated all Estates equally
3. It was difficult to own land
4. members of the Third Estate did not have power in the government

3. Which statement best describes the extent of Napoleon's conquests?
1. his empire spanned most of Europe
2. he conquered present day England and France
3. Italy was not part of his empire
4. Napoleon's empire included parts of Europe, Africa and Asia

4. One reason for the fall of Napoleon's empire was
1. his military strategy during the invasion of present-day Spain
2. his scorched earth strategy
3. his decision to invade Russia
4. his refusal to expand the navy

Proclamation of the National Assembly 1789 (Excerpt)

Besides, since it belongs only to the representatives who have verified their powers, to concur in the formation of the national wish, and since all the representatives so verified should be in this Assembly, it is therefore indispensable to conclude that it belongs to it, and to it only, to interpret and exhibit the general will of the nation; so that between the Throne and this Assembly, there can exist no veto, no negative power.

The Assembly therefore declares, that the common work of National Reform can, and ought to be commenced without delay by the Deputies present, and that they ought to pursue it without interruption, and without obstacles.

5. The Proclamation of the National Assembly was created for the purpose of
1. to create a timeline for the commencement of the national budget
2. allowing King Louis XIV to choose its representatives
3. letting the clergy understand that the French citizens wanted a secular government
4. giving the Third Estate a voice in government through its representatives

6. According to the proclamation the king would not be able to
1. veto a decision of the National Assembly
2. tax the citizens more than 10%
3. allow the nobles to join the assembly
4. live in the Palace of Versailles

7. The creation of the National Assembly was in response to
1. the decree of the Church to forbid divorce
2. the king's refusal to implement reforms
3. the implementation of a new tax system by the nobles
4. a book published by Thomas Hobbes

The Three Estates

8. The point of view of this political cartoon is
1. the Third Estate is propped up with a "cane" of social reforms
2. the Third Estate is carrying the burden of paying for the Second and Third Estates
3. most citizens of the Third Estate are elderly
4. men in France are making the important decisions

9. The caption under the cartoon translates to "we must hope that the game will end soon". The "game" they wanted ended is
1. the Declaration of the Rights of Man
2. the plight of the clergy
3. piggyback rides
4. unfair taxes

10. Which Enlightenment ideals influenced the citizens to revolt against the government?
1. capitalism and free trade
2. freedom of religion and the press
3. shared power of government and natural rights
4. lower taxes and divine right

Nationalism

After the French Revolution, the French felt a great pride in their country. **Nationalism** developed among people that share a language, background and culture. In the 1800s nationalism would help to unify Italy and Germany and cause revolutions in Latin America.

Italy

After the fall of the Roman Empire Italy had been divided into small states. Napoleon's conquest of Italy resulted in some of the Italian states uniting into the Kingdom of Italy. The Congress of Vienna redivided Italy and much of it was under Spanish and Austrian control. Three leaders helped to unify Italy to create one nation.

<u>**Giuseppe Mazzini**</u> formed Young Italy, a nationalist movement. He is known as "the heart" of Italian unification with his writings and ideas.

<u>**Count Camillo Cavour**</u> was the "brains" of the national movement. He shrewdly formed alliances with France and Prussia. He used diplomacy and war to drive Austria out of power.

<u>**Giuseppe Garibaldi**</u> was the "sword", a soldier who led forces and won control of southern Italy. He helped to unite the south with the north to create one Italy.

Germany

Germany was also a group of smaller states. Prussia was the largest and strongest of the states. Prussia set up an economic agreement that encouraged trade amongst the states, unifying it economically.

<u>**Otto von Bismarck**</u> was appointed chancellor of Prussia in 1862. He was a strong leader who helped to unify Germany.

Bismarck believed that the only way to unite Germany was through "blood and iron". He led Prussia into 3 wars. Each time Prussia was strengthened and German states were brought closer together.

In 1871 the Prussian king, William I, brought the German states together. He called himself kaiser, meaning emperor, of Germany.

Latin America

During the 1400s to 1600s, European powers established colonies, settlements controlled by the home country to take advance of local resources, from Canada to South America. The area from Mexico to South America is "Latin America" because   of the "Latin" languages of French, Spanish and Portuguese spoken there.   The series of islands in the Caribbean are the "West Indies," the area originally assumed to be part of India.

Outside control by those who often did not respect the needs of local residents, including because of racism against non-whites, led to a desire for self-rule. This "nationalism" was seen in 1776 when the United States declared their own independence. Enlightenment thought promoting self-government influenced the situation. Also, the attempt of distant powers to retain control over large areas with limited resources also could be problematic.

Haiti

The beginning of the decolonization, the process of colonies in Latin America gaining independence, began in the French controlled colony of Saint-Domingue (now Haiti). After a slave revolt in 1791, the French government (now under French Revolution control) abolished slavery.

Toussaint Louverture, a former slave himself, grew to be the leader of a Haitian independence movement. Napoleon, with plans to at least partially retain slavery, attempted to regain control as part of an American empire, but failed. Louverture was killed in the attempt, but Haiti obtained independence (1804). The French failure also led to the sale of the Louisiana Territory to the United States.

New Spain

The Spanish colonies in America were called "**New Spain**" with **viceroyalties** basic units of government. Local people of Spanish ancestry were "criollos" and "mestizos" were persons of mixed Spanish and Native American ancestry.

Local criollo control in Spanish America underwent a crisis as a result of Napoleon placing his brother in control in Spain. A series of independence movements in Mexico, Central and South America (key leaders: **Simón Bolívar** and **José de San Martín**) occurred into the 1820s. The **Treaty of Cordoba** established Mexican independence, Mexico at that time included California and other surrounding areas.

These movements helped motivate the Monroe Doctrine (1823) in the United States, which opposed additional European colonial involvement in the Americas.

Brazil

Portugal controlled Brazil during colonial times. The Napoleonic invasion of Portugal led to the exile of the Portuguese royal family to Brazil. Brazil in effect became "Portugal in exile" and retained special non-colonial status after the fall of Napoleon. In fact, the son of the Portuguese king eventually declared Brazil independent, and it was officially recognized as such by Portugal in 1825.

. . . I shall tell you with what we must provide ourselves in order to expel the Spaniards and to found a free government. It is union, obviously; but such union will come about through sensible planning and well-directed actions rather than by divine magic. America stands together because it is abandoned by all other nations. It is isolated in the center of the world. It has no diplomatic relations, nor does it receive any military assistance; instead, America is attacked by Spain, which has more military supplies than any we can possibly acquire through furtive [stealthy] means.

When success is not assured, when the state is weak, and when results are distantly seen, all men hesitate; opinion is divided, passions rage, and the enemy fans these passions in order to win an easy victory because of them. As soon as we are strong and under the guidance of a liberal nation which will lend us her protection, we will achieve accord [unity] in cultivating the virtues and talents that lead to glory. Then will we march majestically toward that great prosperity for which South America is destined. Then will those sciences and arts which, born in the East, have enlightened Europe, wing their way to a free Colombia, which will cordially bid them welcome. . . .

— Simón Bolívar, "Reply of a South American to a Gentleman of This Island [Jamaica]," September 6, 1815 (adapted)

1. What is Simon Bolivar's ultimate goal?
1. sensible planning and well-directed actions
2. a united and free South America
3. more military supplies to fight Spain
4. an easy victory

2. What are the historical circumstances of this document?
1. the French Revolution
2. the American Revolution
3. Latin American independence movements
4. mercantilism

3. The following quote, "when success is not assured, when the state is weak, and when results are distantly see, all men hesitate" means
1. Spain is not sure of its dominance over South America
2. talent must be cultivated to learn the science and art of Europe
3. divine magic will not bring success
4. many Latin Americans area hesitant to support independence because they might not win

Excerpt of a speech by Prussian Chancellor Otto von Bismarck

"Prussia's borders according to the Vienna Treaties [of 1814-15] are not favorable for a healthy, vital state; it is not by speeches and majority resolutions that the great questions of the time are decided – that was the big mistake of 1848 and 1849 – but by iron and blood."

4.According to Bismarck, what is necessary to unify Germany?
1. creating a new treaty to replace the Treaty of Vienna
2. a favorable, healthy state
3. military might
4. the use of diplomacy

5. Who is the intended audience of this speech?
1. the French chancellor
2. the European Union
3. the German people
4. the leader of Prussia

6. This painting of a Haitian revolt was led by
1. Simon Bolivar
2. Toussaint Louverture
3. Jose de Saint Martin
4. Napoleon Bonaparte

7. Haiti gained its independence from
1. Spain
2. England
3. Portugal
4. France

The Program of *Count Cavour*, 1846:

The history of every age proves that no people can attain a high degree of intelligence and morality unless its feeling of nationality is strongly developed. This noteworthy fact is an inevitable consequence of the laws that rule human nature. . . .Therefore, if we so ardently desire the emancipation of Italy--if we declare that in the face of this great question all the petty questions that divide us must be silenced--it is not only that we may see our country glorious and powerful but that above all we may elevate her in intelligence and moral development up to the plane of the most civilized nations. . . .This union we preach with such ardor is not so difficult to obtain as one might suppose if one judged only by exterior appearances or if one were preoccupied with our unhappy divisions. Nationalism has become general; it grows daily; and it has already grown strong enough to keep all parts of Italy united despite the differences that distinguish them.

8. According to Count Cavour a driving force to unify Italy is
1. imperialism
2. nationalism
3. militarism
4. pizza

9. Another example of unification during the 19th century is
1. Germany
2. England
3. Portugal
4. France

10. What claim can best be supported based on the passage?
1. A union of people is difficult to attain and leads to unhappy divisions
2. Italy has many differences which must be overcome in order to strive for unity
3. A strong degree of nationality is necessary to achieve a high degree of intelligence and morality
4. We must elevate and develop the achievements of Italian women to achieve unification

The Industrial Revolution (1700s – 1800s)

The Industrial Revolution was a great change in the way products were made. Before the revolution goods were produced at home or in small shops. After the invention of machines goods were mass-produced in factories. The word industrial refers to manufacturing products.

Industrial Revolution Begins in Britain

For a place to industrialize certain things are necessary:
- **Capital**; money to invest
- **Natural Resources**; coal and iron are important raw materials needed to manufacture goods.
- **Labor**; a large population of workers are needed to fun the machines
- **Rivers and roads**; to transport the materials and finished goods

Britain had all these advantages, and the Industrial Revolution began there. It later spread to other countries in Europe and to the United States. There are some countries that a still industrializing in the 21st century.

Inventions - Several important inventions helped to foster the growth of industry.
- The **spinning jenny** was invented by James Hargreaves in 1764. This device allowed workers to produce more than one spool of thread at a time. This is the first step in manufacturing textile (cloth)
- James Kay invented a weaving machine called the **Flying Shuttle** in France in 1733. It allowed thread to be woven into fabric using less labor.
- The **Steam Engine Locomotive** patented by George Stephenson in 1814. This new mode of transportation ran on rails and revolutionized the way goods (and later people) were transported.

Effects of the Industrial Revolution

Building factories and purchasing machines required a large investment of **capital.** Business owners sold **shares** in their companies, or stocks to investors. This process helped to start some of the world's first large corporations.

Before the revolution there were 2 main classes in Europe, the nobles and the peasants. Industrialization helped a larger middle class to emerge. Professionals and shop owners as well as teachers and office workers improved their standard of living.

Thousands of people moved from farms and small towns to cities to work in the new factories. Cities grew very quickly. This urbanization caused working-class people to live in crowded and unsanitary conditions. Without sanitation and sewage systems disease spread.

In the beginning, working conditions in the factories was terrible. Men, women and children worked 12-16 hour days for very little pay in dangerous working conditions.

Many of the initial effects of industrialization were negative. However, the standard of living increased for many. Transportation increased as canals, roads and railroads were built.

The challenges created by the Industrial Revolution gave birth to various solutions. These philosophies were opposed to each other, and each drew followers.

Laissez-Faire Capitalism

Before industrialization, the economic policy in Europe was mercantilism, which called for government regulations. During the Enlightenment a new idea, called laissez-faire, was introduced. Adam Smith wrote the *Wealth of Nations* promoting this system.

Laissez-faire economics stated that government should not regulate and control businesses. Owners should run their companies as they saw fit. The natural forces of supply and demand would control the market and determine prices.

In 1859 a scientist named Charles Darwin concluded that humans and animals evolved over millions of years. The strong, healthy and fastest would survive and have improved offspring. This was called natural selection, or survival of the fittest. Industrialists adopted these ideas to business. Successful businessmen did well because they were naturally better and were more fit to succeed than others. The weaker ones would naturally be weeded out.

Socialism

A German philosopher named Karl Marx studied the effects of the Industrial Revolution. He saw how businessmen got rich from the hard labor of their workers. In his book, The Communist Manifesto, he explained his ideas. According to Marx history was a class struggle between the wealthy and the poor. The capitalists took advantage of the proletariat (working class). He believed the workers would rise up in revolution and take over the capitalist system. Then they would control the means of production, and everyone would share in the profits.

> . . . *Owing to the extensive use of machinery and to division of labor, the work of the proletarians has lost all individual character, and, consequently, all charm for the workman. He becomes an appendage [accessory] of the machine, and it is only the most simple, most monotonous, and most easily acquired knack [skill] that is required of him. Hence, the cost of production of a workman is restricted, almost entirely, to the means of subsistence that he requires for his maintenance, and for the propagation [reproduction] of his race. But the price of a commodity, and also of labor, is equal to its*
> *cost of production. In proportion, therefore, as the repulsiveness of the work increases, the wage decreases. Nay more, in proportion as the use of machinery and division of labor increases, in the same proportion the burden of toil also increases, whether by prolongation [stretching] of the working hours, by increase of the work exacted in a given time, or by increased speed of machinery, etc. . . .*
> Source: Marx and Engels, The Communist Manifesto, 1848

1. Which best describes the point of view of Marx and Engels as the to type of jobs factories offered?
1. they were abundantly available leading to a growing middle class
2. the work was boring and repetitious
3. the production of commodities led to Britain's wealth
4. factories offered good opportunities to low skilled workers

2. During which historical time period was the *Communist Manifesto* published?
1. Industrial Revolution
2. Green Revolution
3. Neolithic Revolution
4. Nationalistic movements

3. What did Marx and Engels believe would be the effect over time of the working conditions described?
1. Factory owners would begin to offer higher wages as an incentive to workers
2. A laissez-faire system would be implemented to improve working conditions
3. the workers would unite and rise up against the factory owners
4. there would be a consolidation of industries causing monopolies

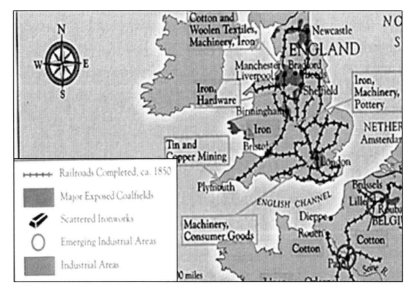

4. Based on the map above one reason the Industrial Revolution began in England was
1. it was an emerging industrial area
2. the English Channel protected trade secrets from spreading
3. an abundance of natural resources
4. easy access to markets of France and Spain

5. An important component of England's successful distribution of goods included
1. an extensive rail system
2. the first postal system
3. copper mining
4. northern tailwinds for ships

Testimony of a teenage girl working in an English coal mine:
Ann Eggley, eighteen years old.—I'm sure I don't know how to spell my name. We go at four in the morning, and sometimes at half-past four. We begin to work as soon as we get down. We get out after four, sometimes at five, in the evening. We work the whole time except an hour for dinner, and sometimes we haven't time to eat

6. As indicated in the testimony above, one effect of the Industrial Revolution was
1. urbanization
2. a surplus of coal
3. capitalism
4. poor working conditions

7. Which of the following was NOT an effect of the Industrial Revolution?
1. Laissez-Faire Capitalism
2. urbanization
3. expanded agricultural opportunities for small farmers
4. new inventions

Year	Population
1761	6,146,000
1781	7,042,000
1801	8,893,000
1821	12,000,000
1841	15,914,000
1861	20,066,000
1881	25,974,000

Before the Industrial Revolution, England and Wales had just over 6 million people. By the end of the Industrial Revolution, England had over 25 million people. Some reasons for the increase was that soap became cheaper so more people could wash germs and bacteria away before infection grew, and cotton was being used more widely which meant that garments were easier to wash.

8. The chart above spans a time period of
1. 100 years
2. 150 years
3. 120 years
4. 130 years

9. According to the information above, 1 cause of the population growth during this time period in England and Wales was
1. better hygiene
2. more advanced farming methods
3. an increase in overall wealth
4. families having more children

10. The increase in population in England was a cause of the Industrial Revolution because
1. it increased the markets for goods
2. labor was needed to work in the factories
3. other European countries experienced a decrease in population during the same period
4. there was a large pool of inventors to create machines

Imperialism

Imperialism is the extension of a nation's power by means of diplomacy or military force, which existed in some form since there were nations. Our concern here is particularly Western European imperialism in Africa and Asia. But, Japan and the United States also had imperialist dreams as these events took place.

Foreign Policy

Foreign policy involves a nation's relationship with other countries. Western European nations from the 1400s and 1600s had a foreign policy of exploring new lands around the world and setting up colonies. Colonies are settlements set up by a home country usually to exploit the resources of the area and provide a market for goods. The United States, for example, started as colonies of Great Britain.

The colonial system included a lot of racism, white Europeans exploiting non-white locals seen as inferior including use of black slavery. This sometimes took a patronizing form ("white man's burden") in which Europeans said they had a duty to control non-whites for their own good. Also, pseudo-scientific arguments were made that argued only the strongest nations naturally would survive and control others. This version of scientific evolutionary thought is "Social Darwinism."

There are various ways for nations to control weaker ones, including without directly setting up colonies. A "sphere of influence" involves economic and political control of an area. Military and economic power, including a weaker nation relying on another to be a market, allowed nations to have spheres of influence throughout the world without needing to extend the resources of colonial rule.

Age of Imperialism

The "Age of Imperialism" is often dated as taking place from the second half of the 19th Century until World War I, largely involving India, China and Africa. Imperialist countries were particularly concerned with profitable raw materials, often having a one-minded focus of exploitation over the needs of the locals. This would have many negative consequences with lingering problems remaining after colonies obtained independence in the years after World War II.

India

The British East India Company was formed in the 17th Century to trade and exploit the resources of India and Asia (such as spices, saltpeter, tea, and opium). It set up trading posts and established a large military presence over the years to control chunks of India. A failed rebellion by Indian soldiers (sepoys) led to direct British rule in the 1850s, which continued until Indian independence in the 1940s.

China

China was in a weakened position for various reasons in the 19th Century, allowing various nations to take advantage. For instance, Great Britain and France fought "opium wars" with China to defend a profitable trade in opium and other goods.

The United States, who gained an overseas empire with the defeat of Spain in the War of 1898, negotiated an "open door" policy in which all nations would have equal trading privileges with China. This would help lead to the end of imperial China in 1912, after a failed anti-imperialist "Boxer Rebellion" a few years before.

Scramble for Africa

The late 19th Century involved a "scramble" of European powers to occupy and divide Africa. This led to the Berlin Conference to negotiate terms of colonization and trade. Belgium, for instance, secured control of the Congo. Imperial disputes and alliances involved here would in time help lead to World War I.

There were also military disputes among European settlers themselves. The Boer War arose between Dutch (Boers or Afrikaners) settlers and the British with Great Britain winning. South Africa was now clearly under British control.

Imperialism in Japan

For 200 years Japan had been isolated from most of the world. Tokugawa shoguns had limited trade with other countries in order to retain their power. This isolation would end with the arrival of an American fleet coming to open trade with Japan.
In 1854 Commodore Matthew Perry led American warships to Japan. His mission was to deliver a letter from the president asking Japan to open its port for trade with the United States. Intimidated by the show of strength from America the shogun signed the Treaty of Kanagawa giving trading rights to the United States.
This treaty was a wake-up call for Japan. The shogun had shown weakness to foreigners by signing the agreement. Some Japanese realized that Japan needed to modernize to protect itself. A rebellion ensured overthrowing the shogun and restoring the emperor to power.

Meiji Restoration

In 1868, after the emperor was restored, began a period known as the Meiji Restoration. Meiji means "enlightened rule". The emperor implemented reforms between 1868 and 1912 that would quickly modernize Japan and create a strong, imperial nation.

Reformers were sent to western countries in Europe to learn new technologies and customs. They returned to Japan with their new knowledge and began industrializing. They built factories. The government developed a banking and postal system. Roads and railroads were built. Their military was expanded and modernized.

"When the missionaries came to Africa they had the Bible and we had the land. They said "Let us pray." We closed our eyes. When we opened them we had the Bible and they had the land." — Desmond Tutu

1. The message of the quote above is
1. Africa is predominantly Christian today because missionaries converted the masses
2. Europeans distracted the African people with religion in order to steal their land
3. Africans sold their land for bibles
4. Desmond Tutu converted to Christianity by reading the bible

2. Desmond Tutu is describing
1. nationalism
2. despotism
3. absolutism
4. imperialism

3. The pizza in the political cartoon symbolizes
1. European spheres of influence in China
2. Europeans dividing a large pizza and not sharing with China
3. Germany and France arguing
4. Chinese nationalism

4. One example of Chinese rebellion against imperialism is
1. Amritsar massacre
2. Salt March
3. Boxer Rebellion
4. Meiji uprising

Excerpt of President Millard Fillmore's letter to the Emperor of Japan
(presented by Commodore Perry on July 14, 1853)

...Commodore Perry is also directed by me to represent to your imperial majesty that we understand there is a great abundance of coal and provisions in the Empire of Japan. Our steamships, in crossing the great ocean, burn a great deal of coal, and it is not convenient to bring it all the way from America. We wish that our steamships and other vessels should be allowed to stop in Japan and supply themselves with coal, provisions, and water. They will pay for them in money, or anything else your imperial majesty's subjects may prefer; and we request your imperial majesty to appoint a convenient port, in the southern part of the Empire, where our vessels may stop for this purpose. We are very desirous of this.

These are the only objects for which I have sent Commodore Perry, with a powerful squadron, to pay a visit to your imperial majesty's renowned city of Yedo: friendship, commerce, a supply of coal and provisions, and protection for our shipwrecked people.

We have directed Commodore Perry to beg your imperial majesty's acceptance of a few presents. They are of no great value in themselves; but some of them may serve as specimens of the articles manufactured in the United States, and they are intended as tokens of our sincere and respectful friendship.

5. One goal of President Fillmore's letter to the emperor was
1. to sell American steamships to the Japanese
2. to purchase specimens not manufactured in the United States
3. be allowed to replenish coal and water for American ships in Japan
4. to purchase land for the purpose of agriculture

6. Which of the following quotes from the document is evidence that the United States was attempting to intimidate Japan during Commodore Perry' visit?
1. "They will pay for them in money, or anything else your imperial majesty's subjects prefer"
2. "we request your imperial majesty to appoint a convenient port."
3. "We have directed Commodore Perry to beg your imperial majesty's acceptance of a few presents"
4. "which I have sent Commodore Perry, with a powerful squadron, to pay a visit..."

7. What can you infer from the presents that were sent to the emperor?
1. Fillmore was showing off products to interest the emperor in trading with the U.S.
2. the emperor had made known his desire for American made products
3. the U.S. president was trying to bribe the emperor
4. Fillmore expected presents in return from the emperor

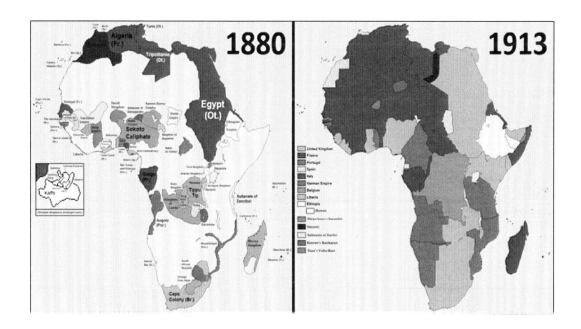

8. Which of the following titles would be most appropriate for the maps above?
1. "The Expansion of South Africa"
2. "Commerce Amongst African Nations"
3. "The Effects of Imperialism on Africa"
4. "African Land Use from 1880-1913"

9. Which conference created the divisions shown in the map?
1. Versailles Conference
2. Berlin Conference
3. Conference of Paris
4. Manchester Conference

10. One effect of the changes shown in the maps above was
1. Europeans divided Africa without consideration to existing alliances
2. natural resources increased in value
3. Egypt's land mass was expanded.
4. Most of Africa converted to Christianity

World War I (1914-1918)

On June 28, 1914, Archduke Franz Ferdinand, heir to the throne of Austria-Hungary, was assassinated in Sarajevo by members of a secret society known as the Black Hand. This would be the spark that started a world war.

Causes (M.A.I.N.)

The seeds of World War I began years before as Europeans began building up their armies and navies, **militarizing** their nation. Western European countries formed **alliances**, organizations of support, to protect each other's interests. Each nation also was actively involved in expanding its power, including being involved in **imperialism** abroad particularly in Africa. Strong feelings of **nationalism** created rivalries and feelings of superiority.

This led to various conflicts with the danger that alliances would cause even a small dispute to become a major unstoppable conflict between the two sides. And, this is what happened in 1914: a dispute between Serbia (allied with Russia) and Austria-Hungary (allied with Germany) led to the **assassination of Archduke Frances Ferdinand** of Austria-Hungary. This was the spark that ignited the war.

On one side, Germany and Austria-Hungary (and the Ottoman Empire) became the "**Central Powers**" and the other Britain, France and Russia (and others such as Japan) became the "**Allied Powers.**"

Stalemate

The fighting in World War I began with Germany invading Belgium on their march toward France. This would become the "Western Front" while fighting in Eastern Europe between Germany and Russia was the "Eastern Front." But, fighting took place throughout the world, including in the Middle East, Africa and in the Atlantic Ocean with German submarines (**U-Boats**) there attacking British shipping.

There soon was a stalemate, a point where neither side could gain the upper hand. The Germans were stopped at the Battle of the Marne (France) and each side dug trenches with a "**no man's land**" between each army. One battle alone (Somme) led to over a million dead and wounded, but little change. Deadly weapons such as poisonous gas just made war more nasty. Airplanes (the German Red Baron a famous fighter pilot) started to be used as well but only so much.

United States Enters

Great Britain used their naval supremacy to blockade, prevent the supply of goods,

Germany. Germany answered by use of submarines, which led to conflict with the United States, whose own shipping was threatened.

Germany in early 1917 took the risk of **unrestricted submarine warfare**, including against non-military targets, which is where the United States drew the line. This led to the United States entering the war, especially after it was discovered (via the British decoding the "**Zimmerman Telegram**") that Germany plotted with Mexico for their support in return for lands lost after the Mexican War.

Russia Leaves

Divisions grew during the war, including in the weakening Austria-Hungarian and Ottoman Empires. Also, civil war arose in Russia (with the assistance of Germany, who helped the communist revolutionary Vladimir Lenin travel there), resulting in the overthrow of Czar Nicholas II. This would eventually lead to communist control of Russia, but in the short run, involved Russia pulling out of the war.

1918

United States "doughboys" (soldiers) would provide fresh troops and resources to the Allied side. Germany had a "Spring Offensive" in 1918 to try to gain the upper hand before this occurred. This failed and the Second Battle of Marne would later be the ultimate turning point for the Allies. On November 11th, 1918, an armistice (agreement to stop fighting) occurred.

The Treaty of Versailles

A treaty at the end of war is written by the victors and World War I was no exception. Britain and France suffered devastating losses and wanted Germany punished. The United States, coming into the war late and geographically distant had different ideas. President Wilson proposed 14 ideas or 14 Points that he wanted.

Ultimately Wilson failed to achieve most of his goals. He was successful in creating an international peace-keeping organization, the **League of Nations**. Congress opposed the United States joining because it feared dangerous alliances in the future. As a result, the United States did not join the League.

1. Which cause of World War 1 is depicted in the political cartoon?
1. Militarism
2. Alliances
3. Nationalism
4. Imperialism

2. The immediate cause of World War 1 was
1. the assassination of Archduke Ferdinand by a Serb
2. the build-up of weapons by European nations
3. appeasement
4. the Zimmerman letter

"The world must be made safe for democracy· Its peace must be planted upon the tested foundations of political liberty· We have no selfish ends to serve· We desire no conquest, no dominion· We seek no indemnities for ourselves, no material compensation for the sacrifices we shall freely make·"—President Wilson on the State of War with Germany during an Address to Congress

3. Why was the world not "safe for democracy" when the U.S. entered World War 1?
1. The Russian Revolution had resulted in a communist government
2. the weapons of World War 1 were too dangerous
3. German aggression against the United States through unrestricted submarine warfare
4. trench warfare

4. One cause of the United States entering World War 1 was
1. Germany's attempt to bring Mexico into the war against the U.S.
2. Germany's attacks on the British
3. Austria's alliance with Serbia
4. France's involvement in the war

Excerpts from the Treaty of Versailles
Article 42: "Germany is forbidden to maintain or construct any fortifications …
Article 45: "As compensation for the destruction of the coal mines in the north of France, and as part payment towards the total reparation due from Germany for the damage…
Article 87: "Germany, in conformity with the action already taken by the Allied and Associated Powers, recognizes the complete independence of Poland, and renounces in her favor all rights and title over the territory [ceded by Germany]."
Article 159: "The German military forces shall be demobilized and reduced as prescribed hereinafter."

5. According to the Treaty of Versailles
1. Germany was allowed to occupy Poland
2. German military forces came under the command of France
3. German fortifications were to be sold to Britain
4. Germany had to pay war damages

6. The historical circumstance surrounding the Treaty of Versailles was
1. the end of World War 1
2. the end of World War 2
3. the end of European imperialism
4. the United States entrance into World War 1

7. One long-term effect of the treaty was
1. France became an economic force in Europe
2. a world-wide economic depression
3. the rise of Hitler as a fascist leader of Germany
4. the end of trench warfare

The Peace Treaty of Brest-Litovsk

Article I· Germany, Austria-Hungary, Bulgaria, and Turkey, for the one part, and Russia, for the other part, declare that the state of war between them has ceased· They are resolved to live henceforth in peace and amity with one another·

Article V· Russia will, without delay, carry out the full demobilization of her army inclusive of those units recently organized by the present Government· Furthermore, Russia will either bring her warships into Russian ports and there detain them until the day of the conclusion of a general peace or disarm them forthwith· Warships of the States which continue in the state of war with the Powers of the Quadruple Alliance, in so far as they are within Russian sovereignty, will be treated as Russian warships·

8. The purpose of the Treaty of Brest-Litovsk was
1. to withdraw Russia from World War 1
2. to demilitarize Russia
3. to increase the warships of Austria-Hungary and Germany
4. allow Germany the use of Russian ports

9. What circumstances led to the Treaty of Brest-Litovsk?
1. the Allied Powers were losing the war
2. Germany's use of submarine warfare
3. the assassination of the Austro-Hungarian heir
4. a civil war in Russia

10. Why would the Central Powers agree to this treaty?
1. Russia offered reparations
2. A major enemy was withdrawing from the war
3. they could focus their attention on the United States
4. Russia's use of poison gas would end

Russian Revolution

First Russian Revolution (1905)

At the turn of the twentieth century Russia faced many problems. A few wealthy nobles owned most of the land. An autocratic ruler, Czar Nicholas II proved to be an unpopular and ineffective ruler.

There were food shortages. Factory workers faced low wages and bad working conditions. Peasant farmers had no hope of owning land. Russia was humiliated by a defeat in a war with Japan. There were waves of protest.

On January 22, 1905, workers marched toward the **czar's** (or "tsar") palace, demanding better working conditions. They were fired upon by soldiers, leading to many deaths, an event labeled "**Bloody Sunday.**" Strikes and riots followed. Worker groups or "soviets" were formed and among the groups involved were communists, following the ideology of Karl Marx.

Czar Nicholas II promised reform, including new representative assemblies (**Dumas**) and a new Russia Constitution. However, there were limited changes and discontent continued.

February Revolution (1917)

During Russia's involvement in World War I protesters, including striking workers, took to the streets in March 1917 (Russia used the Julian calendar, so it was February there). Ordered to attack the protesters, the army itself revolted against the czar, who abdicated (gave up) his throne. He and his family later would be executed.

A temporary or "provisional" government was formed by the Duma. Two groups competed for power, the Petrograd Soviet (representing the workers) and the Provisional Government (the traditional government without the czar).

Bolshevik Revolution

Vladimir Lenin gained leadership of the workers party (**Bolshevik**), promoting a workers' revolution (**communism**) with red symbolizing the blood that would be shed. He promised the people "land, bread and peace". They became known as "the Reds" with those challenging them "the Whites" (representing the imperial forces). Lenin rallied the peasants promising them "bread, peace, land," meaning the end of the war and food for the hungry and land for peasants.

Bolsheviks gained control of the government in November 1917 (**October Revolution**) and signed a peace treaty with Germany withdrawing from World War I. A civil war between red and white forces soon began. After years of violent conflict, the red forces won out in 1923. The workers now said to be in control, Russia was now called the "Soviet Union."

Joseph Stalin

Lenin died in 1924 and Joseph Stalin became the leader. He set in place a "**five-year plan**" to modernize the country, including use of **collective (group-led) farms** and a goal to build factories and improve its industrial output. There was at best mixed success with deadly famines and limited economic development. Stalin ruled as a dictator, blocking all dissent (censorship) and killing hundreds of thousands of assumed opponents (**Great Purge**).

In one part of the Soviet Union, the Ukraine, there was resistance to collective farming. To make an example of them, Stalin ordered all grain and food removed from the Ukraine. No one could leave or bring in food. From 1932 to 1933 millions of Ukrainians starved to death.

1. The intended audience for this political cartoon would be
1. the czar of Russia
2. the clergy of Russia
3. the peasants and workers of Russia
4. the nobles in Russia

2. The point of view of the political cartoon is
1. Vladimir Lenin plans to remove the czar and nobles
2. A Russian street sweeper is protesting for higher wages
3. The czar is excited and willing to allow Lenin to "sweep away" the people
4. Russia is overpopulated and needs to remove part of the population

3. Lenin promised to replace the existing government with
1. a monarchy
2. democratic rule
3. communism
4. fascism

"Ideas are more powerful than guns. We would not let our enemies have guns, why should we let them have ideas." — Joseph Stalin

4. According to the Joseph Stalin quote above
1. freedom of speech must be protected at all costs
2. gun control would be a key component of his policies
3. he did not believe in advanced education
4. people who disagreed with him should be silenced

5. What policy would Joseph Stalin put into place based on this quote?
1. censorship
2. high taxes on guns
3. freedom of religion
4. a one policy platform

6. What caused the mass starvation shown in the headlines?
1. several years of draught caused low farm output
2. inflation caused food prices to soar
3. Stalin seized all the food from the Ukrainians
4. climate change caused late frosts

7. Why was the policy described above implemented?
1. Stalin was prejudiced against the ethnic Ukrainians
2. Stalin punished them for voicing dissent against collective farms
3. Communist policies dictated everyone needed to work in the factories
4. History does not document the reason for the famine

8. The article in the lower left-hand side is titled "Reported Risks Life to Get Photographs Showing Starvation." Why was he in danger for his life?
1. Censorship in the Soviet Union would have caused him to be arrested and executed
2. The famine took place in the coldest part of the winter
3. The photographer was sneaking food into the Ukraine
4. It was illegal to travel from Chicago to the Soviet Union at that time

Actual Industrial production growth of Soviet Union under Stalinist Five-Year Plan (1928)

Industry Production (in millions of tons)

9. The goal of Joseph Stalin's five-year plans were
1. to import less pig iron
2. lower the price of steel
3. to quickly industrialize
4. to double to production of oil

10. According to the chart above was Stalin successful in reaching his goals?
1. No, production decreased
2. Yes, overall production of goods increased
3. Iron ore increased dramatically
4. Production increased but also did the prices

Between the Wars (1918-1939)

The twenty-year period between the two world wars was filled with activity. In hindsight, it might seem that a second world war was inevitable, but that is not how the average person at the time saw it.

World War I Ends

The ceasefire at the end of World War I (armistice) led to peace talks. Germany had to give up territory in Europe and Africa. The Austria-Hungary empire broke apart. And, several new independent countries were formed including Poland, Finland, Yugoslavia, and Czechoslovakia. The Ottoman Empire also broke apart, some parts coming under European control, Turkey becoming independent. Meanwhile, via the Russian Revolution, Russia became the communist Soviet Union.

Weimar Republic (1919-33)

After the war Germany formed the Weimar Republic, but it had a troubled existence. Many thought Germany only lost World War I because of the decisions supported by the new government. The peace terms (Treaty of Versailles), including reparations paid to the victors, were seen as too harsh. Economic difficulties, including the experiences arising out of a worldwide **Great Depression** (economic downturn), worsened the situation.

Growth of Fascism

Economic difficulties helped lead to the growth of **fascism**, a government by dictator with the rights of the people threatened in a variety of ways, an "us vs. them" nationalistic and militaristic mentality arising. There was also a push to use communistic approaches. The Soviet Union, after its revolution was a communist nation under brutal control of Joseph Stalin.

Fascists also gained control in Italy (Mussolini) and Spain (Franco). Franco's forces gained full control after winning the Spanish Civil War in the 1930s. Japan's leadership also grew more fascist, including seizing Manchuria from China, and after winning control of Nanking, being guilty of many heinous civil rights violations there.

Road to War

The **Munich Agreement** (allowing Germany to annex a German populated portion of Czechoslovakia known as the Sudetenland) was not enough to **appease** them. After forming a **non-aggression pact** with the Soviet Union to prevent the Soviets from invading Germany from the west, Germany invaded Poland in September 1939. Meanwhile, Japan pressed its own expansionist campaigns in China and the Pacific. World War II had begun.

Adolf Hitler Speech, 1938 (Excerpt)

Ultimately, the economy of today's empire stands and falls with foreign policy security. It is better to see this in good time than too late.

I therefore consider it the supreme task of the National Socialist leadership to do everything humanly possible to strengthen our military strength. I build on the insight of the German people and especially on his memory.

We have no right to suppose that if Germany ever succumbed to another seizure in the future, its fate would take on a different shape; on the contrary, it is in part even the same men who once threw into the world the great war fire and to endeavor today, as driving forces or as driven agents in the service of international sedition, to increase enmities so as to prepare a new fight.

And above all you, especially my deputies, men of the Reichstag, do not forget one thing:

In certain democracies, it seems that one of the special prerogatives of political-democratic life is the artificially breeding of hatred of the so-called totalitarian states, that is to raise public opinion against peoples that displace others through a flood of partly disfiguring, partly even fictitious reports did not harm people and did not want to harm them, who were at most themselves deprived of grave injustice for decades.

1. Hitler's goal in this speech is to gain support in
1. increasing factory production to improve the economy
2. build up Germany's military
3. to change public opinion about totalitarian states
4. to strengthen prerogatives of political-democratic life

2. Which of the following quotes from Hitler's speech accuses the west of propaganda against Germany?
1. "Ultimately, the economy of today's empire stands and falls with foreign policy security"
2. "I build on the insight of the German people and especially on his memory."
3. "raise public opinion against peoples that displace others through a flood of partly disfiguring, partly even fictitious reports"
4. "who were at most themselves deprived of grave injustice for decades"

3. Which cause of World War 1 is reflected in this speech?
1. Militarism
2. Alliances
3. Imperialism
4. Nationalism

Sections of a speech by Mussolini to the Fascist Grand Council, 7 April 1932, on plans to change the peace terms agreed after World War 1

It suits us, in one way, that GERMANY should re-arm quickly and efficiently in order to offset FRANCE; but on the other hand, so far as we are concerned, we must try to build up ourselves so that we can look GERMANY in the eyes if and whenever the need arises. ......

If the right of re-armament is withheld from the conquered peoples, then there is no reason why GERMANY and the other countries should stay in the League of Nations. And in that case the League of Nations will end with a bang. Which would not be altogether unforeseen by us, for the League of Nations has so far only been an Anglo-French condominium to maintain Anglo-French hegemony (dominance) in the world. ......

Then there are the colonial clauses. Clearly those who have benefited by the peace, will not wish to entertain ideas of this kind. But there is no advantage for us in maintaining the peace as it was formulated at VERSAILLES. It is to our interest to set the Nations and history on the move. ......

4. Mussolini's purpose for proposing to militarize Italy is
1. to intimidate France
2. in order to increase its colonies abroad
3. to be on par with Germany's military capabilities
4. in order to bolster fascism in Italy

5. The League of Nations referred to in the document was
1. an international peacekeeping organization
2. an early condominium complex
3. an economic cooperation between Germany and Italy
4. the peace agreement that ended World War 1

6. The quote *"there is no advantage for us in maintaining the peace as it was formulated at VERSAILLES."* indicates Mussolini is intending
1. to rewrite the Treaty of Versailles
2. increase Italy's colonial powers
3. Side with France against Germany
4. Break some provisions of the Treaty of Versailles

"SHH-HH! HE'LL BE QUIET NOW—MAYBE!"

7. The political cartoon refers to which historical circumstance?
1. the Munich Agreement
2. the Treaty of Versailles
3. the German Soviet Nonaggression Pact
4. the Berlin Conference

8. The point of view of this cartoon is
1. that Europe was taking care of Hitler
2. Chamberlain thinks that Europe needs to stop complaining
3. Europe is hopeful that appeasing Hitler will avoid war
4. Hitler is acting like a baby

> All within the state, nothing outside the state, nothing against the state.
>
> Benito Mussolini

9. Mussolini's description of fascism reflects
1. extreme nationalism
2. a philosophical connection to democracy
3. an openness to communism
4. an alliance with Germany

10. Based on the quote one can infer
1. Mussolini was preparing for war
2. censorship would be one effect of fascism
3. the state must have a large population to succeed
4. cooperation with other nations would take place

World War II (1939-1945)

World War I, "the Great War" was supposed to be the war to end all wars. Unfortunately, it was a factor in many of the problems facing the world in the decades after the armistice. Worldwide depression, the rise of fascist leaders and the Treaty of Versailles would lead the world into a second world war just 20 years after the first.

Road To War

Fascism involves a dictator that suppresses opposition, promotes an extreme form of nationalism and military control and favors expansion of power beyond its borders. The growth of fascism in Germany (Nazi Party under Hitler as "Fuhrer" or leader), Italy (Mussolini) and Japan (Emperor Hirohito with true power in such leaders as Hideki Tojo) ultimately led to World War II.

The Treaty of Versailles punished Germany for World War 1 with reparations, loss of their military and the humiliation of having to accept blame for the war. The Great Depression exacerbated the problems. In this climate a strong leader who promised to return Germany to its former greatness the appointment of **Adolf Hitler** as chancellor of Germany was widely accepted.

All three fascist leaders began expanding their territory by invading other countries. Italy invaded Ethiopia, Japan invaded China and Germany attacked Czechoslovakia. The **Munich Agreement** between France and Britain with Germany allowed Hitler to annex the Sudetenland (part of Czechoslovakia) with the promise that he would stop there.
He did not.

War in Europe

World War II began when Germany invaded Poland in September 1939, leading Great Britain and France ("the Allies") to declare war on Germany.

Poland quickly was defeated by use of a "**blitzkrieg**" (lightning attack), quick attack, which also was used to defeat France in June 1940. By this time, Winston Churchill was prime minister of Great Britain, whose army barely survived a retreat from Dunkirk. Great Britain would suffer "the Blitz," German air attacks, for years to come though the Royal Air Force helped protect the island itself from invasion.

Pearl Harbor

In 1940, Germany, Italy and Japan signed the Tripartite Pact, forming the "Axis" alliance. Japan continued its expansionist policies by invading Indochina, threatening Dutch and British colonial possessions.

The United States, worried about its own territories including the Philippines, Western powers put an embargo (trade blockage) on Japan. This was a serious move against an island nation at war. Japan on December 7, 1941 (which President Roosevelt called a "day that will live in infamy"), attacked the United States naval base at Pearl Harbor. The U.S. declared war on the Axis Powers.

Two Front War

After Nazi Germany controlled Western Europe, it invaded the Soviet Union in June 1941. The Soviet Union, itself a fascist state under Joseph Stalin, had signed non-aggression pacts with Germany and Japan. This set up an "Eastern Front" of the war and later led to a German defeat at Stalingrad, a major turning point in the war. Soviet military control, however, also led to Eastern Europe to be under its influence after the war as well.

A two front war stretched the resources of the Axis Powers in Europe, fighting taking place in Northern Africa, the Mediterranean (Italy) and eventually the "D-Day" invasion of France on June 6, 1944.

The Holocaust

During the war, a **genocide** was taking place. **Antisemitism**, persecution of Jews, had been escalating in Germany before World War 2. German Jews were not allowed to hold government jobs and were forced to wear the Star of David on their arm to identify their religion. The Nazis had devised a Final Solution, a plan to exterminate all Jews. They sent Jewish men, women and children to concentration camps where they were starved and executed. Ultimately 6 million European Jews were killed.

Defeat

Germany fighting two fronts ultimately led to their defeat in May 1945. Shortly after Hitler committed suicide, as Germany's chances by then was hopeless. Italy was defeated in 1943. Victory in Europe (VE Day) only came after years of death and destruction, including a "total war" that targeted civilians as well as military combatants. This includes six million dead in the Holocaust.

The U.S. navy played a significant part in the defeat of Japan, fighting a series of battles such as Midway (1942) to move toward Japan itself. As this occurred, a secret project (**Manhattan Project**) to create a nuclear bomb took place, which ultimately led to two bombs being dropped on Japan (Hiroshima and Nagasaki) in August 1945. Japan surrendered in September 1945, known as VJ Day.

> *"No salvation is possible until the bearer of disunion, the Jew, has been rendered powerless to harm·"* – Adolf Hitler

1. What is Hitler's point of view in this quote?
1. Saving Jewish people will be difficult
2. The Jews have been made powerless in Germany
3. Jews are the cause of problems within Germany
4. The Jewish religion is secondary to Christianity

2. What event took place as a result of this opinion?
1. the rape of Nanking
2. the Holocaust
3. the bombing of Hiroshima
4. alliance of the Axis Powers

Ho Hum! No Chance of Contagion.

3. The message of this political cartoon is
1. the United States escaped many effects of World War 2 because of its location
2. Uncle Same is happy not to catch an outbreak of the mumps in Italy
3. Europe's bed is crowded and the United States could sleep alone
4. Europe was suffering from many diseases at the same time

4. What can be inferred from this cartoon?
1. European nations were embroiled in too many alliances
2. The United States was superior to Europe
3. Geography is an important factor in historical events
4. The United States should have entered World War 2 sooner to save lives

> "Yesterday, December 7, 1941—a date which will live in infamy—the United States of America was suddenly and deliberately attacked by the naval and air forces of the Empire of Japan." – President Roosevelt

5. What event is President Roosevelt referring to in this quote?
1. the Manhattan Project
2. the Munich Agreement
3. Germany's refusal to adhere to the Treaty of Versailles
4. the attack on Pearl Harbor

6. How did the United States respond to this event?
1. they threated to cut off commerce with Japan
2. they entered World War 2
3. they re-asserted their policy of neutrality
4. they held Hitler responsible

7. The atomic bomb shown in the photo is a result of
1. the Manhattan Project
2. the failure of trench warfare
3. Germany's unrestricted submarine warfare
4. The Arizona Project

8. The bomb was dropped
1. on Hiroshima by the Axis Powers
2. on Berlin by the Americans
3. on Hiroshima by the Allied Powers
4. on Berlin by the Allied Powers

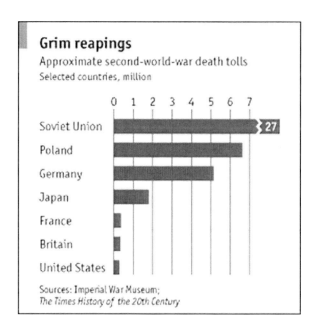

Grim reapings

Approximate second-world-war death tolls
Selected countries, million

Soviet Union	27
Poland	
Germany	
Japan	
France	
Britain	
United States	

Sources: Imperial War Museum;
The Times History of the 20th Century

9. Why did the United States suffer the smallest number of casualties during World War 2?
1. the American air force protected soldiers on the ground
2. the U.S. was geographically separated from the fighting in Europe and entered the war late
3. the U.S. militarized in a larger capacity than the other nations
4. the U.S. was on the side of the Allied

10. In which of the countries listed above did World War 2 begin?
1. Germany
2. the Soviet Union
3. France
4. Poland

The Cold War

After World War II two world superpowers emerged, The United States and the Soviet Union. Each had opposing governments and ideologies. A cold war – distrust and tensions without an open declaration of war – would last for 45 years. There would be several "hot wars" known as proxy wars.

Truman Doctrine

The **United Nations**, an international peacekeeping organization that -- unlike the League of Nations -- the United States joined, was formed as World War II ended. Unfortunately, hopes for world peace clashed with growing divisions between former allies.

The United States provided financial aid to help rebuild Western Europe (**Marshall Plan**), but the Soviet Union rejected such aid, fearing a threat to their independence. President Truman spoke out against communism, his "**Truman Doctrine**" to prevent its spread applied by giving aid to Greece and Turkey. The overall principle also led to the United States involvement in a civil war in Korea to resist communism, which also involved communist controlled China.

Iron Curtain

Winston Churchill, the prime minister of Great Britain, symbolically spoke of an "**iron curtain**" arising to divide communist and non-communist Europe. The Soviet Union was an ally during World War II, but this was an alliance of convenience, underlying conflicts between the two sides never truly going away. Germany itself was divided into two (East, communist and West, democratic) as was its capital city (Berlin).

The Soviet Union formed a defensive treaty with Eastern European nations (**Warsaw Pact**) while Western Europe and the United States formed the National Atlantic Treaty Organization (**NATO**). An actual physical wall (**Berlin Wall**) was built by East Germany to divide its portion from West Berlin, a sign of the suppression of freedoms in communist Europe and fears of the power of the West.

Superpowers

Two competing "superpowers," the United States and Soviet Union, arose with the military, political and economic means to influence world events. Other nations, particularly China, also had significant power, but these two were key players in the Cold War. Each had "satellites," nations which they did not directly rule but had significant power over both politically and economically. This included former colonies which over the years gained independence but had limited power.

Not wishing to directly clash, superpowers often used proxies -- third parties -- to flex their power. **Proxy wars**, such as Korea and Vietnam, not only were significant for the countries themselves, but as superpower conflicts. A basic aim was **containment**, keeping the balance of power at the current status. For instance, the **Cuban Missile Crisis** arose when the Soviet Union started to install missiles in Cuba. There was also a fear that if one nation no longer was allied with a superpower, more would follow, like a series of dominoes (**Domino Theory**).

Detente

Each superpower built up their military, including nuclear capabilities, to safeguard their positions. This led to an **arms race**, a competition for military supremacy. But, again, there was a fear of going too far, of World War III. So, there were also continual attempts at detente, efforts to reduce tension.

End of the Soviet Union

Such efforts continued as years of economic problems and political divisions arose in Eastern Europe. These pressures led to reforms. Two policies, **glasnost** (openness, including greater free speech) and **perestroika** (economic restructuring) were established in the Soviet Union under Mikhail Gorbachev in the 1980s.

Gorbachev's policies allowed some private ownership of business (capitalism) and a decrease in censorship. It also resulted in a weakening of Soviet hold over its satellite nations. Independence movement resulted in 15 separate nations in eastern Europe breaking away from the Soviet Union.

The Berlin Wall was taken down in 1989 and Germany was unified. This was the symbolic end to the Cold War. The Soviet Union itself broke apart in 1991. The Cold War was over.

> Treaty of Friendship, Cooperation and Mutual Assistance Between the People's Republic of Albania, the People's Republic of Bulgaria, the Hungarian People's Republic, the German Democratic Republic, the Polish People's Republic, the Rumanian People's Republic, the Union of Soviet Socialist Republics and the Czechoslovak Republic, May 14, 1955[1]
>
> The Contracting Parties, reaffirming their desire for the establishment of a system of European collective security based on the participation of all European states irrespective of their social and political systems, which would make it possible to unite their efforts in safeguarding the peace of Europe; mindful, at the same time, of the situation created in Europe by the ratification of the Paris agreements, which envisage the formation of a new military alignment in the shape of "Western European Union," with the participation of a remilitarized Western Germany and the integration of the latter in the North-Atlantic bloc, which increased the danger of another war and constitutes a threat to the national security of the peaceable states; being persuaded that in these circumstances the peaceable European states must take the necessary measures to safeguard their security and in the interests of preserving peace in Europe;

1. Which is an accurate title for this document excerpt?
1. North Atlantic Treaty Organization
2. Warsaw Pact
3. Paris Peace Treaty
4. North American Free Trade Agreement

2. The phrase "European collective security " refers to
1. a military alliance
2. an economic alliance
3. a large farm owned collectively
4. Europe's security force

3. The stated purpose for the agreement above is
1. protect again Soviet invasion
2. rebuild Europe after World War 2
3. mutual protection from the North-Atlantic bloc
4. a collective vote for the Paris agreements

The "Marshall Plan" speech at Harvard University, 5 June 1947
Aside from the demoralizing effect on the world at large and the possibilities of disturbances arising as a result of the desperation of the people concerned, the consequences to the economy of the United States should be apparent to all. It is logical that the United States should do whatever it is able to do to assist in the return of normal economic health in the world, without which there can be no political stability and no assured peace. Our policy is directed not against any country or doctrine but against hunger, poverty, desperation and chaos. Its purpose should be the revival of a working economy in the world so as to permit the emergence of political and social conditions in which free institutions can exist.

4. The historical circumstances of the Marshall Plan speech was
1. Post-World War 2
2. Post-Cold War
3. World War 2 economic alliances
4. The rise of capitalism

5. Marshall's purpose in wanting to give economic aid to Europe was
1. to create a military alliance with Britain and France
2. to invest post-war profits in Europe
3. to avoid political stability
4. to prevent the spread of communist governments

6. This political cartoon is depicting tensions during
1. the Cuban Missile Crisis
2. the Vietnam War
3. the Korean War
4. the domino effect

7. Why is President Kennedy's finger near the button on the table?
1. to help him win the arm wrestle with Khrushchev
2. to symbolize his willingness to use nuclear weapons
3. to protect the rules of the wrestling match
4. to show Khrushchev that's he's "playing fair"

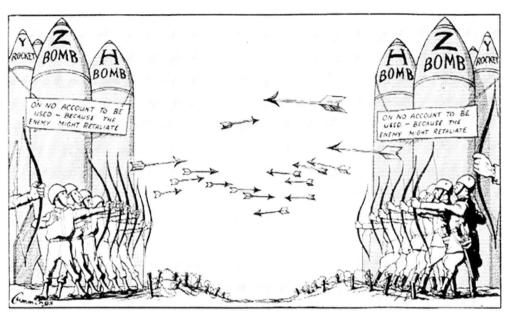

8. The soldiers are fighting with arrows
1. to recreate a Civil War battle
2. because the hydrogen bombs behind them have not been fully tested
3. because the use of atomic weapons would be too devastating
4. to create a fair fight

9. Which is the best title for the political cartoon shown above?
1. *Bombs Away!*
2. *The Impact of Many Arrows*
3. *U.S. and Soviets in a Dead Heat*
4. *Mutual Deterrence of Mutual Destruction*

From Stettin in the Baltic to Trieste in the Adriatic, an iron curtain has descended across the Continent. Behind that line lie all the capitals of the ancient states of Central and Eastern Europe. Warsaw, Berlin, Prague, Vienna, Budapest, Belgrade, Bucharest and Sofia, all these famous cities and the populations around them lie in what I must call the Soviet sphere, and all are subject in one form or another, not only to Soviet influence but to a very high and, in many cases, increasing measure of control from Moscow.

10. Which best describes Churchill's phrase, "an iron curtain has descended across the Continent"?
1. the isolating effect of the Adriatic Sea
2. an invisible but powerful division between east and west Europe
3. the inability for easter Europe to see what was taking place in western Europe
4. the ability of western Europe to protect eastern Europe

Chinese Revolution

Republic Era (1912-1948)

After the fall of the Qing dynasty Sun Yat-sen became the first President of the Republic of China in 1912. However, China was divided with many areas controlled by local warlords. After World War I a communist party developed in China. Mao Zedong became a leader in the movement.

Civil War (1927-1949)

Chiang Kai-shek, now leader of the government, went after communists once he defeated the warlords. This led to a ten year (1927-1936) civil war between the two groups, stopped only when Japan invaded the country. In 1934 the communists had a long retreat ("**Long March**") that was seen as an act of solidarity that cemented Mao Zedong's leadership of the communists.

Once Japan was defeated, the civil war started again, the nationalists with support of the United States and the communists supported by the Soviet Union. The communists gained control of the capital (Beijing) in 1949, declaring a "**People's Republic of China**." The nationalists fled from the mainland to the island of Taiwan, still recognized as the true leaders of the country by the United States until 1979.

People's Republic (1949-Present)

Mao Zedong was now the leader of the with the official ideology known as "Maoism." A collection of his sayings were collected in the **Little Red Book**. Opposition was crushed.
In an effort to modernize China, the **Great Leap Forward** was announced (1958), a policy of rapid industrial growth and agricultural collectivization. Not being ready for such large changes so quickly, the result was famine, leading to millions of deaths.

Cultural Revolution

In the 1960s Mao encouraged a social and political "**cultural revolution**" to revive communist ideals. Red Guards, largely made of students, led the way. Opponents – mainly professionals such as teachers and lawyers -- were suppressed, either killed or sent to farms to be "re-educated" with the right ideology.

Post-Mao

President Nixon visited China in the 1970s, helping to cool United States and Chinese relations. Mao ruled China until dying in 1976.

Deng Xiaoping took power in 1978 and China underwent additional economic reforms, now supporting more private business. He instituted a one-child policy to control the overpopulation in China. Student protests in **Tiananmen Square** (1989), suppressed by the government, showed there continued to be problems.

> Who are our enemies? Who are our friends? This is a question of the first importance for the revolution. The basic reason why all previous revolutionary struggles in China achieved so little was their failure to unite with real friends in order to attack real enemies. A revolutionary party is the guide of the masses, and no revolution ever succeeds when the revolutionary party leads them astray. To ensure that we will definitely achieve success in our revolution and will not lead the masses astray, we must pay attention to uniting with our real friends in order to attack our real enemies. To distinguish real friends from real enemies, we must make a general analysis of the economic status of the various classes in Chinese society and of their respective attitudes towards the revolution.
>
> "Analysis of the Classes in Chinese Society" by Mao Zedong (March 1926)

1. This excerpt from Mao's "Little Red Book" explains that previous revolutions failed due to lack of support from
1. the emperor
2. Mao Zedong
3. communists
4. the peasants

2. How did Mao separate friends from enemies?
1. *by social classes*
2. *by religion*
3. *by their political affiliations*
4. *by their location in China*

3. *Mao's ideas were inspired by*
1. *Deng Xiaoping*
2. *Adam Smith*
3. *Karl Marx*
4. Chiang Kai-shek

Tiananmen Square Massacre Eyewitness

"Despite the menacing tank treads, no one fled. The tanks lost this first battle of willpower and courage. The first tank screeched to a halt 'so suddenly that the streets shuddered, and the top half of the tank lurched forward.' Eventually, the tanks fired tear-gas bombs at the crowds to disperse them. They then mowed down the protesters who were fleeing the choking yellow smoke, and killed at least a dozen people on the spot. Five young protesters were killed at the southwest corner of Liubuko Junction. Two of them were crushed onto bicycles, their corpses mangled together with the bikes."

4. The historical circumstances surrounding the Tiananmen Square Massacre was
1. the Long March
2. students protesting for democratic reforms
3. implementation of the Great Leap Forward
4. collectivization

5. The effect of the protests in 1989 were
1. *immediate reforms in economic policy*
2. *decreased censorship in China*
3. *democratic reforms*
4. *human rights violations*

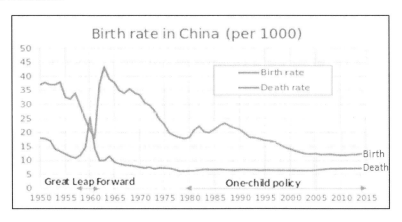

6. Based on the chart above, what was one effect of the Great Leap Forward?
1. decreased birth rate and increased death rate
2. decreased birth and death rates
3. increased birth rate and decreased death rate
4. increased birth and death rates

7. What was a cause of the one child policy?
1. Mao's cultural revolution led to an increased birth rate
2. The Great Leap Forward increased farm production
3. Deng Xiaoping wanted to reduce China's population
4. Birth control became legal in China

8. Mao implemented the Cultural Revolution
1. to increase the average income
2. to foster acceptance by the bourgeoise
3. to implement new social reforms
4. to reignite communist ideals in China

9. Who led the Cultural Revolution in China?
1. Students
2. Professors
3. the elite
4. the original followers of Mao

10. Based on the propaganda poster how would the Cultural Revolution happen?
1. through building new schools
2. by forging new relationships between the provinces
3. by force
4. through humanitarian efforts

Decolonization

European countries for hundreds of years had economic and political power over people in Africa and Asia. Weakened by World War II, they would be forced to give up control and grant independence to imperialized nations.

India

Great Britain deemed India as the "Jewel in the Crown" of a world empire, control arising back in the 17th Century with the British East India Company. In the late 19th Century, the **Indian National Congress** was formed and demands for local self-government grew as well.

Mohandas Gandhi arose as leader for independence. He developed a form of **nonviolent resistance (satyagraha)** to British rule. This included **civil disobedience**, peaceful opposition to what are argued to be unjust laws, such as the **Salt March** in 1930 to protest British's salt monopoly on collection of salt and a salt tax that particularly burdened the Indian poor. He also promoted boycotts of British goods, including producing and wearing homespun cloth.

Independence (and Partition)

Independence came in 1947, Lord Mountbatten was the last British viceroy (colonial representative of the British monarch).   But it was not of a united India.

Gandhi opposed the "two nation theory" that British India must be divided into two nations because of religious divisions between Hindus and Muslims. But divisions were too great to form a single nation.

Muhammad Ali Jinnah became the first leader of **Pakistan,** a Muslim majority nation, at first consisting of eastern and northwestern zones of British India. **Jawaharlal Nehru**, an ally of Gandhi in the independence movement, became the first prime minister of India. Gandhi himself was murdered by a Hindu nationalist shortly afterwards, being blamed for being too sympathetic to Muslims.

Pakistan Divided

The partition of India led to much hardship, including refugees and religious based violence. Also, a border dispute between India and Pakistan involving the **Kashmir** region led to a year long war and conflict that continues to this day.

North Africa

The end of each world war included efforts in support of self-determination, the right of local self-government. **Egypt** won independence from Great Britain after World War I. Italy gave up control of **Libya** as part of their surrender terms after World War II. The **Pan-African Congress** also was formed, bringing together political and intellectual African leaders, in support of African interests.

Central Africa

The "**Scramble for Africa**" in the late 19th Century was particularly focused in Central Africa and often involved bloody conflict to obtain European control of the areas. Traditional borders were often not respected, and the local peoples were harshly treated. This later led to some particularly ugly battles for independence as well as unstable and/or dictatorial regimes which continued to cause deep problems for the African people. Problems linger to this day.

Decolonization in Asia

The burdens of World War II made it harder for European nations to hold onto their overseas empires. Despite the challenges, France did not want to give up control of Algeria in Northern Africa and their possessions in Indochina (Cambodia, Laos and Vietnam). Both areas eventually obtained their independence after extended violent conflicts. Vietnam was divided into two and conflict would continue into the 1970s.

BOMBAY, SUNDAY

The great test has come for "Mahatma" Gandhi, the Indian Nationalist leader, in his efforts to obtain the complete independence of India from British rule. Wading into the sea this morning at Dandi, the lonely village on the Arabian Sea shore, Gandhi and his followers broke the salt monopoly laws and so inaugurated the campaign of mass civil disobedience. There was no interference by the authorities, although a detachment of 150 police officers had been drafted into Dandi and a further force of 400 police was at Jalalpur.

The actual breaking of the salt monopoly law was witnessed by a large crowd who gathered at the seashore. Surrounded by about 100 volunteers—including those who had made the 200-mile march from Ahmedabad,—Gandhi waded into the sea and bathed. Pots were then filled with seawater and boiled or left in the sunshine and the salt residue sprinkled on the ground. Gandhi was hailed by Mrs. Sarojini Naidu, the Indian poetess, as "the lawbreaker." . . .

— The Manchester Guardian, April 7, 1930

1. Which historical event is described in the reading above?
1. Amritsar Massacre
2. the Salt March
3. the Long March
4. Bloody Sunday

2. The form of protest practiced in this event is
1. boycott
2. hunger strike
3. sit-in
4. civil disobedience

3. Gandhi's motive for this event was
1. to gain independence from Britain
2. to gain independence from France
3. to gain cheaper salt for the Indian people
4. to gain notoriety

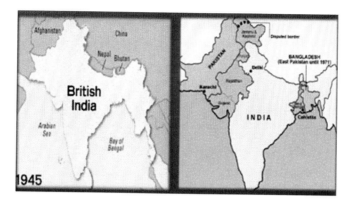

4. The best title for these maps is
1. *The Geography of India*
2. *The British Imperial Empire*
3. *The Partitioning of India After Independence*
4. *The Creation Of Pakistan*

5. The creation of Pakistan and Bangladesh were caused by
1. tensions between Muslims and Hindus
2. tensions between the British and the Indians
3. British insistence for a Hindu nation
4. geographic boundaries separating the Indian people

A DYING COLONIALISM by Frantz Franon (Excerpt)
On November 1, 1954, a small group of Algerian leaders launched an armed struggle, breaking with a whole pattern of negotiation and procrastination established by the old leaders. In a very short time, they had the entire population behind them. The decision to take arms did not spring full-blown from the heads of this handful of leaders. They simply interpreted what was already there in the population as a whole. And the people, in turn, were influenced by revolutions in the rest of the world. In 1949 China tipped decisively and definitively the balance of world power in favor of revolution.

6. One advantage of the Algerian leaders in their struggle for independence was
1. *support of the old leaders*
2. *support of the United States*
3. *support of the mainstream population*
4. *support of Gandhi*

7. Which term best supports the quote, "And the people, in turn, were influenced by revolutions in the rest of the world."?
1. mass immigration
2. ethnocentrism
3. genocide
4. cultural diffusion

W. E. B. Du Bois to
Charles Evans Hughes,1 U.S. Secretary of State
NEW YORK, June 23, 1921

Sir:
In 1919 there was held in Paris the first Pan-African Congress. I am enclosing the resolutions which were passed by that Congress. These resolutions were brought to the attention of Colonel House of the American Peace Commission and received his general approval.

A second Pan-African Congress will be held in August and September at the time and place indicated by the bulletins enclosed. I am writing to appr[i]se you of these facts because of some public misapprehension of our aims and purposes. The Pan-African Congress is for conference, acquaintanceship and general organization. It has nothing to do with the so-called Garvey movement and contemplates neither force nor revolution in its program. We have had the cordial cooperation of the French, Belgian and Portuguese governments and we hope to get the attention and sympathy of all colonial powers.

If there is any further information as to our objects and plans which you would wish to have I will be very glad to write further or to come to Washington and confer with any official whom you might designate. I am, sir, with great respect
Very sincerely yours,
W. E. B. DU BOIS

8. The Pan-African Congress was created
1. to enable African nations to work toward self-rule
2. to engage in economic sanctions against the United States
3. Secretary of State Hughes to attend the next conference
4. force Egypt to allow access to the Suez Canal

9. What was the purpose of this letter to Secretary of State Hughes?
1. to make him aware of DuBois' attendance at the conference
2. to assure him the conference was not radical or militant
3. to invite the secretary of state to the next conference
4. to have the secretary of state veto the resolutions passed

10. Why did DuBois mention the French, Belgian and Portuguese governments?
1. to assure the American government their allies were cooperating with the conference
2. in order to put pressure on the United States to attend
3. to identify the nations as imperialists
4. to entice the secretary to call them

The Middle East

Geography

The Middle East is the region bordering the eastern end of the Mediterranean Sea (including Egypt) to the nation of Iran. Egypt is in Northern Africa, but the Middle East is mainly in the continent of Asia, with the Sinai Peninsula connecting Egypt and Asia. Over recent years, multiple military conflicts arose in the Persian Gulf.

Economically, the region is particularly known for its oil reserves. Multiple nations formed the **Organization of the Petroleum Exporting Countries (OPEC).** Oil is not only the source of money and power in places like Saudi Arabia but gives the region significance beyond its borders.

Three religions also were founded there, Judaism, Christianity and Islam, still causing deep divisions. Islam is the primary religion in the region, while Israel is a Jewish nation. The people in the area are mainly Arab, pan-Arabism being support of a unified Arabian nation and culture. Israel and Iran are two exceptions.

The Creation of Israel

Modern day Israel, a Jewish state, was established in 1948 with the opposition of the surrounding Arab countries and Palestinians living on the land. This led to multiple military conflicts over the years. Israel, with the help of its allies (including the United States) prevailed in these wars. Today Israel still controls "occupied territories" in Israel.

The Iranian Revolution

Modern day Iran was established after World War I as a **secular** (non-religious) state with the leadership by a shah. The shah (leader) grew unpopular and ultimately was overturned in the late 1970s (Iranian Revolution).

Religious leadership, led by Ayatollah Khomeini, took over the country. The new conservative **theocratic** (religiously led) nation had harsh consequences for women's rights and other liberties. The Iranian Revolution was also quickly followed by a long-lasting war with Iraq as well as continuing bad relations with the United States.

Terrorism

Terrorism is the unlawful use of violent resistance to gain political ends and has in modern times been a lasting problem in the region. Terrorism often victimizes average civilians, causing terror in their day-to-day lives. It is a tool used when normal military practices are not possible, because a group doesn't have the control of the state. A major cause of terrorism is religious ideology, including a violent **jihad** (struggle) against perceived enemies of Islam.

The Arab Spring

Beginning in 2010 there was a wave of pro-democracy protests that took place in the Middle East and North Africa. Most nations at the time were ruled by authoritarian regimes. The first nation to experience an uprising was in Tunisia, followed quickly by Egypt. Both countries quickly overthrew their leaders.

Inspired by their success many other nations fought for democratic reforms. Not all saw success. toppled their regimes in quick succession, inspiring similar attempts in other Arab countries. Not every country saw success.

A major cause of the Arab Spring was the advent of social media. Groups were now able to quickly communicate and share information.

Pact of the League of Arab States, March 22, 1945

With a view to strengthen[ing] the close relations and numerous ties which bind the Arab States,
And out of concern for the cementing and reinforcing of these bonds on the basis of respect for the independence and sovereignty of theme Stated,
And in order to direct their efforts toward[s] the goal of the welfare of all the Arab States, their common weal, the guarantee of their future and the realization of their aspirations
And in response to Arab public opinion in all the Arab countries,

Have agreed to conclude a pact to this effect and have delegated as their plenipotentiaries (representative) those whose names are given below:
Who, after the exchange of the credentials granting them full authority, which were found valid and in proper form, have agreed upon the following:

Article 1.
The League of Arab States shall be composed of the: independent Arab States that have signed this Pact.

Every independent Arab State shall have the right to adhere to the League. Should it desire to adhere, it shall present an application to this effect which shall be filed with the permanent General Secretariat and submitted to the Council at its first meeting following the presentation of the application.(2)

Article 2.
The purpose of the League is to draw closer the relations between member States and co-ordinate their political activities with the aim of realizing a close collaboration between them, to safeguard their independence and sovereignty, and to consider in a general way the affairs and interests of the Arab countries.

1. The purpose for forming the League of Arab States was
1. to control the oil in the area
2. to form a security alliance
3. to implement new social reforms
4. to create a welfare state

2. What are the necessary credentials to join the league?
1. a nation's main language must be Arabic
2. they must appoint a secretariat to attend meetings
3. they must be an independent Arab state and present an application
4. they must be a founding member in good standing

3. Who can you infer would NOT be invited to join the League of Arab States?
1. Israel
2. Iraq
3. Saudi Arabia
4. Lebanon

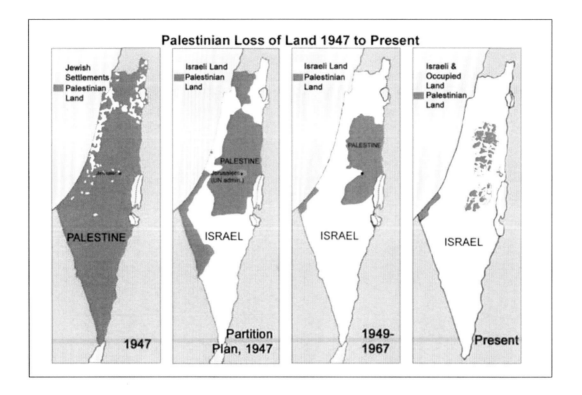

Palestinian Loss of Land 1947 to Present

4. Prior to the creation of Israel
1. the land called Palestine did not exist
2. there were no Jewish people living in the area
3. there were several Jewish settlements in Palestine
4. a partition took place

5. How was Israel created?
1. the United Nations partitioned Palestine and created a Jewish state
2. through a constitutional amendment
3. they bought the land from the Palestinians
4. the United Nations discovered the holy land in Palestine

6. What was an effect of the wars after 1947 between the Palestinians and the Jews?
1. the Treaty of Paris was signed
2. the Palestinians claimed more of the land
3. Many of the Jewish people fled
4. Israel controlled more of the land that was once Palestine

MEET THE NEW BOSS ... SAME AS THE OLD BOSS ...

7. The point of view of this political cartoon about the Iranian Revolution is
1. the ayatollah is better able to keep peace in Iran
2. the revolution is still going on
3. there continues to be civil rights violations
4. Iran has not modernized its military

8. One inference that can be made from this cartoon is
1. the reforms that are fought for are not always realized
2. one effect of revolutions is economic problems
3. the shah of Iran had used diplomacy to try and make change
4. the United States was an ally of the shah

 Noman Al-Husayn @noman_husayn · Aug 27

#Egypt #arabspring #economics #progress When inflation exceeds a populations ability to maintain then democratic reform is required

9. The tweet above indicates that Egypt was
1. trying to hold fair elections
2. overpopulated
3. not participating in the Arab Spring
4. facing economic hardships

10. One cause of the Arab Spring spreading so quickly was
1. poor administration in Arab nations
2. the use of social media to spread ideas
3. Mr. Al-Husayn's ability to finance the uprisings
4. efforts by the United States to encourage the protests

Latin America (Post World War 2)

After 1945 (end of World War 2) many Latin American nations have experienced political and economic problems.

Argentina

In 1946 Juan Perón gained power in Argentina after a military coup (overthrow). He brought economic stability to the country by limiting foreign owned businesses and promoting **import substitution** (when local manufacturers produce goods to replace imported products). He was also a repressive dictator.

In 1976 another military government took power. The new government targeted groups they believed were against the government. They tortured and killed thousands of people in what was called the "dirty war". As many as 20,000 people went "missing" during this time. Most were young people. Their mothers organized a silent march every week for over thirty years holding pictures of their missing children.

In 1983 elections were held in Argentina and voters returned a democratic government to power. This new government worked to restore human rights and control the military. However, economic problems persisted.

Nicaragua

For decades, the **Somoza** family governed Nicaragua. Their anti-communist stand made them allies of the United States.

In 1979 a nationalistic communist group called **Sandinistas** overthrew the Somozas. **Daniel Ortega** was made the new leader. He introduced socialist policies. In the 1980s a counterrevolutionary group called the **Contras** arose hoping to overthrow the Sandinistas. The United States supported the contras as opponents to communism. A civil war ensued.

The civil war led to many deaths and hurt the economy. In 1990 a compromise was reached. The Sandinistas handed over power to a freely elected president. Nicaragua continued its economic struggles.

Mexico

After the Mexican Revolution one political party, the Institutional Revolutionary Party controlled the government for over 70 years. There were problems that caused periodic protests in the country.

Unequal income distribution – a small group of Mexicans controlled most of the wealth and did not want reforms.

<u>Population Growth and Poverty</u> – There was a sharp increase in the population and not enough land to grow food for all the people.

<u>Urban Growth</u> – Many peasants moved to the cities. Slums grew and there was a shortage of jobs.

In 2000 the National Action Party won elections. President Calderon began a military crackdown on drug cartels. The drug lords responded with daily murders making the streets unsafe.

NAFTA

In the 1990s the 3 countries in North America, Canada, the United States and Mexico entered into a trade agreement called the **North American Free Trade Agreement** (NAFTA). The goal was to lower trade barriers, such as tariffs and encourage more business between the 3 countries.

The trade agreement had unequal effects. Some businesses invested in Mexico, helping their economy. Other manufacturers were hurt by U.S. competitors.

Panama

In the 1980s a growing drug problem in the United States led to investigations as to where the drugs were coming from. The leader of Panama, Manuel Noriega, was suspected by U.S. officials of helping drug cartels smuggle drugs into the United States. United States troops entered Panama and arrested Noriega.

The Panama Canal

In the early 1900s the Panama Canal had been constructed by the United States in order to connect the Atlantic and Pacific Oceans for trade. The United States retained control over the land near the canal. In 1977 Panama and the United States signed an agreement to gradually turn control over to Panama. In 2000 Panama once again had complete control over the area.

Memorandum of Torture and Disappearance in Argentina, U.S. State Department:

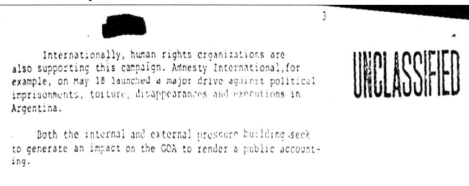

Internationally, human rights organizations are also supporting this campaign. Amnesty International, for example, on May 18 launched a major drive against political imprisonments, torture, disappearances and executions in Argentina.

Both the internal and external pressure building seek to generate an impact on the GOA to render a public accounting.

UNCLASSIFIED

1. According to this previously classified document, the United States was
1. engaging in diplomacy with the government of Argentina
2. aware of human rights violations taking place in Argentina
3. forming an alliance with Amnesty International
4. assessing the impact on the GOA (government of Argentina)

2. One long-term effect of the actions taken by the Argentinian government is
1. a yearly gathering of the mothers of the missing youth
2. ongoing economic sanctions against Argentina
3. an increased ability for CIA operatives to monitor governmental actions in Argentina
4. increased funding for Amnesty International

> **Mexico's Institutional Revolutionary Party (IRP)**
> The party was born in 1929 after years of post-revolutionary instability and maintained power for 7 decades. It survived through a vast political machine that enveloped Mexican life, using patronage and sweetheart deals to tame unions, bureaucrats, peasant groups and intellectuals. At the same time, it kept the media and dissidents largely silenced through coercion or force.

3. One method used by the IRP to retain power was
1. trying to hold fair elections
2. instituting democratic reforms
3. paying off opponents
4. censorship

4. In order to be re-elected the IRP engaged in
1. activities to keep various groups of Mexicans satisfied
2. bribing the clergy for their support
3. union busting tactics
4. celebrating extended holidays such as Valentine's Day

In 1903, after Columbia refused to approve a treaty to grant a strip of land across the isthmus of Panama for the purpose of building a canal, President Theodore Roosevelt supported a revolution in Panama. Negotiating with the new government of Panama was successful. However, Roosevelt then had to persuade Congress to fund the canal project.

5. In order to build the Panama Canal President Roosevelt needed the approval of
1. the Supreme Court and Congress
2. his cabinet and Congress
3. the Panamanian government and Congress
4. the landholders around the isthmus

6. How did President Roosevelt achieve support of the Columbian government?
1. He bribed the public officials in Columbia
2. He took advantage of pollical upheaval in the country
3. He gained approval for the treaty by appealing to the citizens of Columbia
4. He sent ambassadors to use diplomacy

7. The point of view of the political cartoon is
1. the elephant does not want to walk but the teddy bear is helping him
2. the Panama Canal is a deal that was destined to fail
3. President Roosevelt will be able to persuade the Republican party to agree to the deal
4. President Roosevelt is "pushing" the democrats to move forward

8. The North American Free Trade Agreement (NAFTA) referred to in the cartoon is
1. an economic alliance between Mexico, the United States and Canada
2. a military alliance between Mexico, the United States and Canada
3. an agreement that trade would be free in North America
4. a promise to increased tariffs in North America to help their prosperity

9. The author of the political cartoon is sending the message that NAFTA
1. hurt the Mexican economy
2. lowered Christmas sales in North America
3. created problems for some industries and locations
4. does not believe in Santa Claus

10. Which conclusion can be inferred from the political cartoon?
1. the elves don't want to relocate
2. NAFTA had an uneven effect on the economy
3. the goals of an economic alliance are never met
4. NAFTA was bad for all parties involved

International "Hot Spots"

North Korea and South Korea

Between 1950 and 1953 North and South Korea engaged in a civil war. The war ended with a permanent division creating 2 nations, North Korea and South Korea. South Korea has since built a strong global economy.

Post-war North Korea is run by a communist dictator known as supreme leader. It suffers from economic sanctions imposed because it violates international laws. The isolated country suffers from famine. North Korea still hopes to unite the nation under communist rule and spends large sums on military. It became a nuclear power in 2007, periodically testing missiles, causing fear in South Korea and the rest of the world.

Israel and Its Neighbors

After Israel gained independence in 1948 a series of wars ensured between Israel and Palestinians who were living there, as well as with neighboring states. Cease-fire peace talks in 2005 led Israel to withdraw soldiers from Gaza and parts of the West Bank (areas occupied by the Palestinians). In 2006 Palestinians elected a group called Hamas to lead. This political party is known for its anti-Israel policies. Hamas carried out attacks using terrorist methods, such as suicide bombers.

In an attempt to end attacks by Hamas Israel and the adjacent nation of Egypt closed Gaza's borders. The Palestinians responded by digging tunnels between Egypt and Gaza. Israel launched a series of attacks. Hamas retained control over Gaza and wants to create a traditional Islamic society. The region is an ongoing area of tension.

The Iraq War

After Iraq invaded Kuwait in 1990 they were forced out during the Persian Gulf war the nation was required to destroy any nuclear and biological weapons. To ensure compliance the United Nations would send inspectors into Iraq.

In the late 1990s Saddam Hussein, Iraq's leader, refused to allow further inspectors into the country. After failed diplomatic attempts the United States and Britain staged air strikes.

There are 2 sects of Muslims, Sunnis, and Shiites. Living in Iraq is also an ethnic group, the Kurds. Saddam Hussein was a Sunni Muslim. He tortured and killed Shiites and Kurds.

In 2007 the United States invaded Iraq, without the support of the United Nations. Saddam Hussein was captured and found guilty of crimes against humanity and executed in an international court.

1. Based on the political cartoon you can infer that
1. the United Nations is delivering "fake news"
2. China is supporting the United Nations' claims against North Korea
3. China is an ally of North Korea
4. The United Nations has been spying on China

2. A challenge faced by the United Nations depicted in the cartoon is
1. diplomacy does not usually work
2. North Korea is a difficult member of the United Nations
3. it is underfunded
4. it's difficult to get its member to agree on a problem

Hamas Covenant (Excerpt)

"[Peace] initiatives, and so-called peaceful solutions and international conferences are in contradiction to the principles of the Islamic Resistance Movement... Those conferences are no more than a means to appoint the infidels as arbitrators in the lands of Islam... There is no solution for the Palestinian problem except by Jihad (holy war). Initiatives, proposals and international conferences are but a waste of time, an exercise in futility." (Article 13)

3. According to the Covenant, Hamas is NOT a proponent of
1. diplomacy
2. jihad
3. a two-state solution in Palestine
4. throwing infidels out of Palestine

4. Based on the excerpt above, Hamas believes that they
1. had to go to war to reach their goals
2. were the arbitrators of the lands of Islam
3. must begin an initiative in order to succeed
4. should resist war at all costs

Areal View of Eastern Asia at Night

5. Based on the picture above which statement is true?
1. North Korea is twice as large as South Korea
2. Large parts of North Korea do not have electricity
3. North Korea is spying on South Korea
4. North Korea is closer to Japan than South Korea

6. One assumption that can be made from the photo is
1. that North Korea is not industrialized
2. that South Korea is not industrialized
3. North Korea is very good at preserving energy consumption
4. South Koreans can see more stars at night

> The people's army should always maintain a highly agitated state and be equipped with full fighting readiness so as to smash the enemies with a single stroke if they make the slightest move and achieve the historic cause of the fatherland's reunification.
> Kim Jong-un, Supreme leader of North Korea

7. Based on the quote above Kim Jong-un's foreign policy is
1. neutrality
2. diplomacy
3. militarism
4. economic alliances

8. One goal of Kim Jong-un, as stated in the quote above, is
1. to institute democratic reforms
2. to create an alliance with South Korea for mutual gain
3. to agitate its enemies
4. to unify North and South Korea

IRAQ WAR	
Casualties	Costs
189,000: Direct war deaths	$5,000: Amount spent per second
4,488: U.S. service personnel killed directly.	$350,000: Cost to deploy one American military member.
32,223: Troops injured	$490 billion: Amount in war benefits owed to war veterans.
134,000: Civilians killed directly.	$7 trillion: Projected interest payments due by 2053 (because the war was paid for with borrowed money).
- Business Insider (Mar 20, 2013)	

9. Based on the statistics from Business Insider the Iraq War
1. relied heavily on the use of air attacks
2. will cost the American taxpayers for a long time to come
3. costs were constrained by Congress
4. limited the war benefits to veterans

10. According to the chart, casualties of the Iraq War
1. included Iraqi civilians, American and allied troops that died
2. did not consider soldiers that were injured in the line of duty
3. included the death of over 100,000 Iraqi citizens
4. were higher than losses of World War 1

Human Rights Violations

Cambodian Genocide

During 1951 Cambodia, a small Asian country next to Vietnam, gained independence. A communist group called the Khmer Rouge gained power. Their leader was Pol Pot, a brutal dictator

Between 1975-1979 the Khmer Rouge killed almost 2 million Cambodians (over 20% of the population). Pol Pot instituted what he called "year 0" to reset all policies and the way of life in Cambodia. He wanted all citizens to be farmers and drove everyone who was living in the cities out to the countryside. Anyone who resisted was killed. Famine killed millions more.

Apartheid in South Africa

Apartheid (separation) was formerly established in 1948 by the National Party. The policy of Apartheid included a range of social and legal laws to separate people into racial groups: white (19%), black (68%), colored (10%) and Indian (3%). Apartheid was a system of minority white rule.

Apartheid included residential segregation of non-whites into separate townships that were often shantytowns. Passes or identification papers were required for travel and work. Many blacks, Asians, and other people of color were forced out of their homes and into regulated areas called "homelands."

Resistance

Black South Africans formed a group that became known as the African National Congress (ANC) to protest racial oppression. Various non-violent means were used over the years including breaking the laws deemed unjust, known as civil disobedience.

However, in time, more violent protests arose as well. Nelson Mandela formed a violent wing of the ANC and was imprisoned for 27 years starting in 1962 for his actions. Protests continued and news coverage spread throughout the world. Over time worldwide opposition formed against apartheid policies in South Africa.

Ending Apartheid

FW de Klerk's election as president in 1989 started the road to the end of apartheid, including the release of Nelson Mandela from prison. A new constitution was ratified and in 1994 an election was held in which all people of color could vote. Mandela became the president of South Africa.

Rwandan Genocide

There are 2 main ethnic groups in Rwanda, the Hutus and the Tutsis. During the time that Rwanda was imperialized by Belgium the Tutsis, who were thought to look more European, were put in positions of power. Some Tutsis acted superior to the Hutu and treated them disrespectfully.

After Rwanda gained its independence the **Hutus and the Tutsis** fought for power. During the 1990s tensions between the two ethnic groups increased.

On April 6, 1994, Hutu President Habyarimana was assassinated when his plane was shot down. The Hutus blamed the Tutsis. This began the **genocide** (exterminating a group of people) of the **Tutsi** people in Rwanda.

In the period of 100 days 800,000 Tutsis were slaughtered, Thousands of women were raped. The United Nations failed to admit that genocide was taking place and therefore did not send in troops to stop the slaughter. This is an example of genocide and a major human rights violation.

> *Consolee Nishimwe, survivor of the Rwandan Genocide*
> Things started to change way before 1994, even before I was born.
> Tutsis had always been discriminated against and most of them went
> into exile while those who remained in the country were sometimes
> denied certain services. I started to experience this discrimination
> when I joined school as a young girl. However, the situation got worse
> when we started hearing local radio stations calling Tutsis
> "cockroaches" and "snakes," explaining how they were going to kill us.
> And then the genocide happened.

1. According to Consolee Nishimwe's testimony which statement is true?
1. There was occasional discrimination of Tutsis in Rwanda
2. Hutus were forced into exile
3. Discrimination of Tutsis was longstanding
4. Tutsis fought back violently against the genocide

2. One way in which the Hutus spread hate propaganda against the Tutsis was
1. newspapers
2. radio
3. social media
4. email

> "Better to kill an innocent by mistake
> than spare an enemy by mistake."
> -- Pol Pot

3. Who is the enemy Pol Pot is speaking of?
1. anyone who does not support communism in Cambodia
2. the Japanese
3. his main opponent in the election
4. the Chinese

4. Pol Pot's stand against his political enemies could best be compared to
1. Joseph Stalin
2. Zeng Xiaoping
3. the Dalia lama
4. Winston Churchill

Widescale Genocides

Place	Years	Death Toll (Estimated)	Circumstances
Turkey	1915-1918	1,500,000	Ethnic cleansing
Soviet Union	1932-1933	7,000,000	Purges & forced famine
China (by Japan)	1937-1938	300,000	Chinese civilians
Germany	1938-1945	6,000,000	Concentration camps
Cambodia	1975-1979	2,000,000	Purges & concentration camps
Rwanda	1994	800,000	Ethnic cleansing

5. Based on the chart above, one can conclude
1. the Rwandan genocide had the least casualties
2. the Holocaust was the first major genocide to take place
3. the genocides took place on all continents
4. the genocides spanned the 20th century

6. Which ethnic group was the victims of the ethnic cleansing in Rwanda?
1. Hutus
2. Tutsis
3. Twi
4. all of the above

7. The largest death toll in the shortest period of time was in
1. the Soviet Union
2. Germany
3. Cambodia
4. Turkey

Apartheid Legislation

The Population Registration Act, of 1950, required all residents to be classified as colored (European and African mixed or Asian), native (Bantu people), or white. Identity cards were issued and a registry for the entire country was initiated.

The Prohibition of Mixed Marriages Act, of 1949, made it illegal for blacks and whites to marry.

The Separate Registration of Voters Act, of 1951, removed colored South Africans to from the regular voter rolls and placed on separate rolls where they would only be allowed to vote for white South Africans to represent them in the House of Assembly, the South African Senate and on the Cape Provincial Council.

The Bantu Authorities Act, of 1951, set up government-appointed leaders and authorities in territorial areas where blacks were forced to live.

The Pass Laws Act of 1952 required black South Africans over the age of 16 to carry a passbook identification everywhere at all times.

8. The Pass Laws Act was discriminatory because
1. they identified each person's race
2. only Black South Africans were required to carry them
3. minors under the age of 18 were required to carry them
4. blacks and whites could not marry

9. Which law was aimed at denying black South Africans the right to vote in general elections?
1. Bantu Authorities Act
2. Pass Laws Act
3. Population Registration Act
4. Separate Registration of Voters Act

10. All of these apartheid laws were written
1. to ensure that Black South Africans paid the most taxes
2. to ensure the white minority maintained power in South Africa
3. to keep white South Africans from carrying passbooks
4. to help the government keep track of its population

The World Today (1980-Present)

Modern Economic Trends

Industrialization first developed in Britain and spread to the United, the rest of Europe, Japan and Australia. Industrial nations are wealthier nations. This led to an unequal distribution of wealth in the world. Emerging economies, countries that are beginning to industrialize quickly, are still far behind in amassing wealth for their people.

Economic Interconnectedness

Countries have been trading with each other for years. But advancements in technology and transportation have increased trade and communication dramatically. This interaction with each other is known as **globalization**.

Globalization has led to opportunities. It has helped developing countries progress faster. It also resulted in more pollution and encourages companies to make goods through cheap labor overseas.

There were many organizations created to improve trade and stimulate economic growth. The **European Union** was established to reduce trade barriers. It created a new currency, the Euro that was adopted by most European nations.
The **North American Free Trade Agreement** (NAFTA) is a similar economic alliance. The United States, Mexico and Canada agreed to remove **tariffs** to increase trade in North America.

Arab Spring

The Arab Spring was a series of pro-democracy rebellions that spread through the Arab world. It started in December of 2010 when a young Tunisian vendor set himself on fire to protest unfair treatment by officials. Social media and television made the event public for all to see. This quickly led to other uprisings.

Social media in Egypt played a large role in ousting President Mubarak's government. Videos and tweets calling for protests went viral and citizens took to the streets. In 2012 Egyptians elected their first democratically chosen president.
The Arab Spring spread to other nations as well. Libya, Syria and Yemen all experienced uprisings and political disruption.

Modern Science and Technology

Scientists have worked to improve farming technology. This has resulted in an increase of food production. New fertilizers help to enrich the soil and pesticides decrease the loss of crops to pests. Scientists have developed hardier grains, increasing the harvest capabilities. These efforts have led to what's been called the **Green Revolution**. The improvements in agriculture have allowed some countries, such as India, to double their food output.

The Information Age

The most revolutionary change in modern history has been the **Computer Revolution**. Before the 1990s computers were huge machines that filled a large room and worked slowly. The development of the silicon chip enabled computers to shrink in size and become more affordable.

Widespread access to computers led to the **Information Revolution**. Suddenly enormous amounts of information was available to businesses and people. Ideas, opinion and information could be shared worldwide. Social media, such as Facebook and Twitter connected friends and families across the globe. Social and political change, such as the **Arab Spring**, was fueled by social media.

Medical Technology

After World War 2 there have been amazing advancements in medicine. People now live longer, and infant mortality rates have decreased. Antibiotics and vaccines have wiped out diseases such as smallpox in most places. Organ transplants have saved lives.

New challenges have also arisen in medicine. In the 1980s a disease called AIDS (acquired immune deficiency syndrome) killed millions. Pandemics, such as the Avian influenza (bird flu) spread throughout Asia, Europe and the Middle East. The COVID virus caused a worldwide pandemic killing millions.

The Environment

Pollution is the contamination of air, soil and water. It's harmful to humans, animals and plant life. Factories and cars emit pollution into the air. Fertilizers and chemicals poison water sources.

Scientists are concerned about the depletion of the ozone layer, gases that protect the earth from the ultraviolet rays of the sun. This layer is becoming thinner due to the use of chemical pollutants.

Climate Change

Another concern has been the gradual increase in global temperatures. Abnormal cold has also been detected. Many scientists believe that this is caused by the **greenhouse effect**, when warm air is trapped in the lower atmosphere. Causes are thought to be burning fossil fuels (such as coal), the use of chlorofluorocarbons (CFCs) and the destruction of forests. In 2015 the United Nations held a convention on climate change and authored a treaty. The **Paris Agreement** is a legally binding international treaty on climate change. Its goal is to limit global warming. In total 192 nations and the European Union signed the agreement, including China and the United States.

1. The message of this political cartoon is
1. putting coal in stockings at Christmas lowers self esteem
2. the use of fossil fuels is a major cause of the greenhouse effect
3. coal is a nonrenewable resource and should be controlled
4. the use of reindeer increase carbon emissions

2. In order to reduce the effects of global warming scientists advocate
1. electric cars
2. solar power
3. wind power
4. all of the above

WORLD BANK GROUP PRESIDENT JIM YONG KIM
We welcome the historic agreement that has just been reached in Paris. The world has come together to forge a deal that finally reflects the aspiration, and the seriousness, to preserve our planet for future generations
We called for strong ambition, for remarkable partnerships, for mobilization of finance, and for implementation of national climate plans. Paris delivered. Now the job becomes our shared responsibility.

3. Jim Yong Kim's point of view of the Paris Agreement
1. reflects concern as to its efficacy
2. is glad that the responsibility fell to Paris
3. believe the changes in the agreement need to wait for future generations
4. believes it is a positive turning point for the environment

4. According to Jim Yong Kim how will the Paris Agreement be implemented?
1. through economic alliances
2. through military alliances
3. through franchising solar businesses
4. by each country working independently

M. S. Swaminathan (Indian agricultural scientist)

Exploitive agriculture offers great dangers if carried out with only an immediate profit or production motive. The emerging exploitive farming community in India should become aware of this. Intensive cultivation of land without conservation of soil fertility and soil structure would lead, ultimately, to the springing up of deserts. Irrigation without arrangements for drainage would result in soils getting alkaline or saline. Indiscriminate use of pesticides, fungicides and herbicides could cause adverse changes in biological balance as well as lead to an increase in the incidence of cancer and other diseases, through the toxic residues present in the grains or other edible parts.

Unscientific tapping of underground water will lead to the rapid exhaustion of this wonderful capital resource left to us through ages of natural farming. The rapid replacement of numerous locally-adapted varieties with one or two high-yielding strains in large contiguous areas would result in the spread of serious diseases capable of wiping out entire crops, as happened prior to the Irish potato famine of 1854 and the Bengal rice famine in 1942.

Therefore, the initiation of exploitive agriculture without a proper understanding of the various consequences of every one of the changes introduced into traditional agriculture, and without first building up a proper scientific and training base to sustain it, may only lead us, in the long run, into an era of agricultural disaster rather than one of agricultural prosperity.

5. M.S. Swaninathan is warning against what type of agricultural practices?
1. the use of ocean water for irrigation which creates too much salt in the soil
2. using farming strategies that do not consider its environment impact
3. traditional agriculture
4. the growing of cash crops

6. One past result of exploitive agriculture, according to Swaninathan, has been
1. famine
2. overproduction of specific crops
3. communal farms
4. increased immunity to pesticides

7. One solution identified by Swaninathan is
1. conserving soil fertility to avoid desertification
2. tapping the natural water supply
3. increase the use of fungicides to improve crop production
4. the initiation of modern farming techniques

8. According to the political cartoon, one impact of the Arab Spring has been
1. Egypt was the first country to "spring"
2. Egyptian President Mohamed Morsi was deposed
3. Libyan and Syria's leaders are looking to take over Egypt
4. Egyptian President Mohamed Morsi "rose" in power

9. Which of the following best defines the Arab Spring?
1. pro-Islamic uprisings that took place in the Middle East
2. a consolidation of power in the Middle East and North Africa
3. a rapid increase in oil production and profits in Middle Eastern countries
4. pro-democracy protests and uprisings that took place in the Middle East and North Africa

10. One cause of the Arab Spring's rapid expansion was
1. modern reforms in Tunisia
2. new prodemocratic newspaper publications
3. the availability of social media
4. the availability of resources to fund the uprisings

CRQ Set 1 Directions: Analyze the documents and answer the short-answer questions that follow each document in the space provided.

Base your answer to question 1 on Document 1 below and on your knowledge of social studies.

Document 1

What is the Third Estate?
Everything.

What has it been until now?
Nothing.

What will it become?
Something.

Emmanuel-Joseph Sieyès
1748-1836

In January 1789, Emmanuel-Joseph Sieyès wrote his pamphlet "Qu'est-ce que le tiers état?" (translated "What is the 3rd Estate?")

1. Explain the historical circumstances that led Emmanuel-Joseph Sieyes to write this pamphlet.

_____

_____

_____

Constructed Response Questions Sets

Base your answer to question 2 on Document 2 below and on your knowledge of social studies.

Document 2

The Ambiguous Legacy of the Revolution

. . . However, the majority of Europeans and non-Europeans came to see the Revolution as much more than a bloody tragedy. These people were more impressed by what the Revolution accomplished than by what it failed to do. They recalled the Revolution's abolition of serfdom, slavery, inherited privilege, and judicial torture; its experiments with democracy; and its opening of opportunities to those who, for reasons of social status or religion, had been traditionally excluded.

One of the most important contributions of the French Revolution was to make revolution part of the world's political tradition. The French Revolution continued to provide instruction for revolutionaries in the 19th and 20th centuries, as peoples in Europe and around the world sought to realize their different versions of freedom. Karl Marx would, at least at the outset, pattern his notion of a proletarian revolution on the French Revolution of 1789. And 200 years later Chinese students, who weeks before had fought their government in Tiananmen Square, confirmed the contemporary relevance of the French Revolution when they led the revolutionary bicentennial parade in Paris on July 14, 1989.
. . .

Source: Thomas E. Kaiser, University of Arkansas, encarta.msn.com/encyclopedia

2. Identify the point of view of Thomas E. Kaiser of the French Revolution.

_____

_____

_____

Base your answer to question 3 on **both** Documents 1 and 2 and on your knowledge of social studies.

Cause—refers to something that contributes to the occurrence of an event, the rise of an idea, or the bringing about of a development.

Effect—refers to what happens as a consequence (result, impact, outcome) of an event, an idea, or a development.

3 Identify **and** explain a cause-and-effect relationship associated with the historical developments in documents 1 and 2. Be sure to use evidence from **both** documents 1 and 2 in your response.

_____

_____

_____

_____

_____

CRQ Set 2 Directions: Analyze the documents and answer the short-answer questions that follow each document in the space provided.

Base your answer to question 1 on Document 1 below and on your knowledge of social studies.

Document 1

A map depicting the range of Soviet missiles, if launched from Cuba. (photo curtesy of the Central Intelligence Agency.)

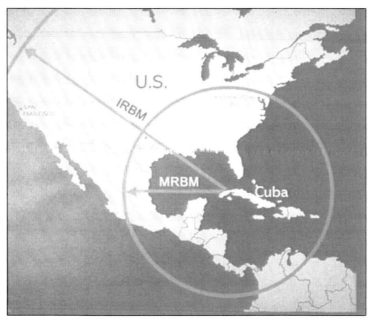

IRBM = intermediate range ballistic missile
MRBM = Medium-range ballistic missile

4. Explain the geographic context for the historical development/event shown on the map.

_____

_____

_____

Document 2

RADIO AND TELEVISION ADDRESS TO THE AMERICAN PEOPLE ON THE NUCLEAR TEST BAN TREATY, JULY 26, 1963 (Excerpt)

President John F. Kennedy:

Nevertheless, this limited treaty will radically reduce the nuclear testing which would otherwise be conducted on both sides; it will prohibit the United States, the United Kingdom, the Soviet Union, and all others who sign it, from engaging in the atmospheric tests which have so alarmed mankind; and it offers to all the world a welcome sign of hope. For this is not a unilateral moratorium, but a specific and solemn legal obligation. While it will not prevent this Nation from testing underground, or from being ready to conduct atmospheric tests if the acts of others so require, it gives us a concrete opportunity to extend its coverage to other nations and later to other forms of nuclear tests. This treaty is in part the product of Western patience and vigilance. We have made clear--most recently in Berlin and Cuba--our deep resolve to protect our security and our freedom against any form of aggression. We have also made clear our steadfast determination to limit the arms race. In three administrations, our soldiers and diplomats have worked together to this end, always supported by Great Britain. Prime Minister Macmillan joined with President Eisenhower in proposing a limited test ban in 1959, and again with me in 1961 and 1962. But the achievement of this goal is not a victory for one side--it is a victory for mankind. It reflects no concessions either to or by the Soviet Union. It reflects simply our common recognition of the dangers in further testing.

5. Based on this excerpt, what is President Kennedy's point of view on the Nuclear Ban Treaty?

_____

_____

_____

Similarity—tells how something is alike or the same as something else.
Difference—tells how something is not alike or not the same as something else.
6. Using evidence from **both** Documents 1 and 2 and your knowledge of social studies:
 a) Identify a similarity **or** a difference between the map of Soviet missiles in Cuba and Kennedy speech on the Nuclear Ban Treaty.
 b) Explain the similarity **or** difference you identified using evidence from both documents.

_____

_____

_____

_____

_____   _____

CRQ Set 1 Directions: Analyze the documents and answer the short-answer questions that follow each document in the space provided.

Base your answer to question 1 on Document 1 below and on your knowledge of social studies.

Document 1

Selected African Colonies and Their Exports

African Colony (European Colonizer)	Resources Exported	Industrial or Economic Use
Angola (Portugal)	cotton palm oil and palm-kernel oil coffee and sugar	fabrics soap and candles; some food products food processing
Congo Free State (King Leopold of Belgium)	rubber palm oil and palm-kernel oil ivory	waterproof clothes, tires, electrical insulation soap and candles; some food products handles, piano keys, billiard balls
French West Africa (France)	gum palm oil and palm-kernel oil cotton peanuts, bananas, coffee, cocoa	cosmetics, drugs, food products soap and candles; some food products fabrics food processing
Rhodesia (Great Britain)	copper zinc lead coal	coins, metal alloys, electrical wiring metal alloys, rust protection metal alloys, ammunition fuel
South Africa (Great Britain)	gold diamonds	banking, national currencies, jewelry jewelry, industrial cutting tools
Tanganyika (Germany)	sisal coffee rubber cotton	rope and twine food processing waterproof clothes, tires, electrical insulation fabrics

1. Explain the historical circumstances that led to the trade of resources listed above.

_____

_____

_____

Document 2

But should not the German nation who is fundamentally so very capable, so seaworthy, so industrially and commercially minded ... successfully pave the way for this new course? ... It would be wise if we Germans would learn about colonial skills from our Anglo-Saxon [British] cousins and would begin-in a friendly competition-to strive after them. When the German Reich centuries ago was at the peak of the states in Europe, it was the Number One trade and sea power. Should the New German Reich wish to prove and maintain its newly won position of power for a long time, it will have to take up the same culture-mission and delay no longer to acknowledge its colonial task anew.

Source: Freidrich Fabri, Does Germany Need Colonies? 1879. Note: Freidrich Fabri (1824-1891) has been called the "father of the German colonial movement."

2. Explain Freidrich Fabri's point of view in the document above.

_____

_____

_____

Base your answer to question 3 on **both** Documents 1 and 2 and on your knowledge of social studies.

     Cause—refers to something that contributes to the occurrence of an event, the rise of an idea, or the bringing about of a development.

     Effect—refers to what happens as a consequence (result, impact, outcome) of an event, an idea, or a development.

3. Identify **and** explain a cause-and-effect relationship associated with the historical developments in documents 1 and 2. Be sure to use evidence from **both** documents 1 and 2 in your response.

_____

_____

_____

_____

_____

CRQ Set 2 Directions: Analyze the documents and answer the short-answer questions that follow each document in the space provided.

Base your answer to question 4 on Document 1 below and on your knowledge of social studies.

Document 1

Declaration of the Rights of Man - 1789

Articles:

1. Men are born and remain free and equal in rights. Social distinctions may be founded only upon the general good.

2. The aim of all political association is the preservation of the natural and imprescriptible rights of man. These rights are liberty, property, security, and resistance to oppression.

3. The principle of all sovereignty resides essentially in the nation. No body nor individual may exercise any authority which does not proceed directly from the nation.

4. Liberty consists in the freedom to do everything which injures no one else; hence the exercise of the natural rights of each man has no limits except those which assure to the other members of the society the enjoyment of the same rights. These limits can only be determined by law.

5. Law can only prohibit such actions as are hurtful to society. Nothing may be prevented which is not forbidden by law, and no one may be forced to do anything not provided for by law.

6. Law is the expression of the general will. Every citizen has a right to participate personally, or through his representative, in its foundation. It must be the same for all, whether it protects or punishes. All citizens, being equal in the eyes of the law, are equally eligible to all dignities and to all public positions and occupations, according to their abilities, and without distinction except that of their virtues and talents.

7. No person shall be accused, arrested, or imprisoned except in the cases and according to the forms prescribed by law. Any one soliciting, transmitting, executing, or causing to be executed, any arbitrary order, shall be punished. But any citizen summoned or arrested in virtue of the law shall submit without delay, as resistance constitutes an offense.

4. Explain the historical circumstances that led to the publication of the Declaration of the Rights of Man.

_____

_____

_____

Base your answer to question 5 on Document 2 below and on your knowledge of social studies.

Document 2

> ## The following was a decree (law) passed by the National Assembly and considered the beginning of the Reign of Terror
>
> The Law of Suspects (17 September 1973)
>
> 1. Immediately after the publication of the present decree, all suspects within the territory of the Republic and still at large, shall be placed in custody.
>
> 2. The following are deemed suspects:
>   1--those who, by their conduct, associations, comments, or writings have shown themselves partisans of tyranny and enemies of liberty;
>   2--those who are unable to justify, in the manner prescribed by the decree of 21 March, their means of existence and the performance of their civic duties;
>   3--those to whom certificates of patriotism have been refused;
>   4--civil servants suspended or dismissed from their positions by the National Convention or by its commissioners, and not reinstated, especially those who have been or are to be dismissed by virtue of the decree of 14 August;
>   5--those former nobles, together with husbands, wives, fathers, mothers, sons or daughters, brothers or sisters, and agents of the émigrés, who have not constantly domonstratcd their devotion to the Revolution,

5. Explain the purpose of the National Assembly creating this law.

_____

_____

_____

Similarity—tells how something is alike or the same as something else.
Difference—tells how something is not alike or not the same as something else.

6. Using evidence from **both** Documents 1 and 2 and your knowledge of social studies:
 a) Identify a similarity **or** a difference between the ideas shown in the Declaration of the Rights of Man and the decree of the National Assembly.
 b) Explain the similarity **or** difference you identified using evidence from both documents.

_____

_____

_____

_____

_____

CRQ Set 1 Directions: Analyze the documents and answer the short-answer questions that follow each document in the space provided.

Base your answer to question 4 on Document 1 below and on your knowledge of social studies.

Document 1

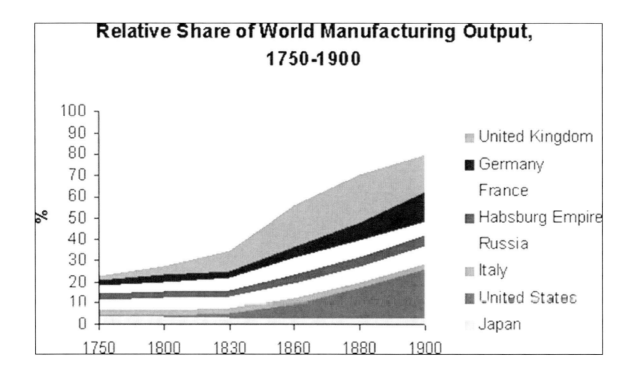

1. Explain the historical circumstances that the led to the results of the manufacturing output shown above.

_____

_____

_____

Base your answer to question 5 on Document 2 below and on your knowledge of social studies.

Document 2

... Every great town has one or more slum areas into which the working classes are packed. Sometimes, of course, poverty is to be found hidden away in alleys close to the stately homes of the wealthy. Generally, however, the workers are segregated in separate districts where they struggle through life as best they can out of sight of the more fortunate classes of society. The slums of the English towns have much in common—the worst houses in a town being found in the worst districts. They are generally unplanned wildernesses of one- or two-storied terrace houses built of brick. Wherever possible these have cellars which are also used as dwellings. These little houses of three or four rooms and a kitchen are called cottages, and throughout England, except for some parts of London, are where the working classes normally live. The streets themselves are usually unpaved and full of holes. They are filthy and strewn with animal and vegetable refuse. Since they have neither gutters nor drains the refuse accumulates in stagnant, stinking puddles. Ventilation in the slums is inadequate owing to the hopelessly unplanned nature of these areas. A great many people live huddled together in a very small area, and so it is easy to imagine the nature of the air in these workers' quarters. However, in fine weather the streets are used for the drying of washing and clothes lines are stretched across the streets from house to house and wet garments are hung out on them. ...

Source: Friedrich Engels, The Condition of the Working Class in England, W. O. Henderson and W. H. Chaloner, eds., Stanford University Press

2. Explain Engels' purpose in writing *The Condition of the Working Class.*

_____

_____

_____

Turning point—is a major event, idea, or historical development that brings about significant change. It can be local, regional, national, or global.

3. Using evidence from **both** Documents 1 and 2 and your knowledge of social studies:
 a) Identify a turning point associated with the historical developments related to both Documents 1 **and** 2.
 b) Explain why the historical developments associated with these documents are considered a turning point. Be sure to use evidence from both Documents 1 **and** 2 in your response.

_____

_____

_____

_____

_____

CRQ Set 2 Directions: Analyze the documents and answer the short-answer questions that follow each document in the space provided.

Base your answer to question 4 on Document 1 below and on your knowledge of social studies.

Document 1

The Nazi-Soviet Non-Aggression Pact of 1939

"Eastern Frontier" is written on the path

SOMEONE IS TAKING SOMEONE FOR A WALK

4. Explain the geographic circumstances that led to the Nazi-Soviet Non-Aggression Pact shown in the political cartoon above.

_____

_____

_____

Base your answer to question 5 on Document 2 below and on your knowledge of social studies.

Document 2

British Prime Minister Neville Chamberlain gave this speech to the House of Commons on September 1st, 1939, just hours after Hitler's troops had invaded Poland.

I do not propose to say many words tonight. The time has come when action rather than speech is required. Eighteen months ago in this House I prayed that the responsibility might not fall upon me to ask this country to accept the awful arbitrament of war. I fear that I may not be able to avoid that responsibility.

But, at any rate, I cannot wish for conditions in which such a burden should fall upon me in which I should feel clearer than I do today as to where my duty lies.

No man can say that the Government could have done more to try to keep open the way for an honorable and equitable settlement of the dispute between Germany and Poland. Nor have we neglected any means of making it crystal clear to the German Government that if they insisted on using force again in the manner in which they had used it in the past we were resolved to oppose them by force.

Now that all the relevant documents are being made public we shall stand at the bar of history knowing that the responsibility for this terrible catastrophe lies on the shoulders of one man, the German Chancellor, who has not hesitated to plunge the world into misery in order to serve his own senseless ambitions...

Only last night the Polish Ambassador did see the German Foreign Secretary, Herr von Ribbentrop. Once again he expressed to him what, indeed, the Polish Government had already said publicly, that they were willing to negotiate with Germany about their disputes on an equal basis.

What was the reply of the German Government? The reply was that without another word the German troops crossed the Polish frontier this morning at dawn and are since reported to be bombing open towns. In these circumstances there is only one course open to us.

5. What was Neville's purpose in addressing the House of Commons on September 1, 1939?

_____

_____

_____

Base your answer to question 3 on **both** Documents 1 and 2 and on your knowledge of social studies.

      Cause—refers to something that contributes to the occurrence of an event, the rise of an idea, or the bringing about of a development.

      Effect—refers to what happens as a consequence (result, impact, outcome) of an event, an idea, or a development.

6. Identify **and** explain a cause-and-effect relationship associated with the historical developments in documents 1 and 2. Be sure to use evidence from **both** documents 1 and 2 in your response.

_____

_____

_____

_____

_____

ENDURING ISSUES ESSAY #1

This question is based on the accompanying documents. The question is designed to test your ability to work with historical documents. Some of these documents have been edited for the purposes of this question. As you analyze the documents, take into account the source of each document and any point of view that may be presented in the document. Keep in mind that the language and images used in a document may reflect the historical context of the time in which it was created.

Directions: Read and analyze each of the five documents and write a well-organized essay that includes an introduction, several paragraphs, and a conclusion. Support your response with relevant facts, examples, and details based on your knowledge of social studies and evidence from the documents.

An enduring issue is a challenge or problem that has been debated or discussed across time. An enduring issue is one that many societies have attempted to address with varying degrees of success.

Task:

> • Identify **and** define an enduring issue raised by this set of documents
> • Argue why the issue you selected is significant **and** how it has endured across time
> **In your essay, be sure to**
> > • Identify the enduring issue based on a historically accurate interpretation of at least three documents
> > • Define the issue using relevant evidence from at least three documents
> > • Argue that this is a significant issue that has endured by showing: – How the issue has affected people or has been affected by people – How the issue has continued to be an issue or has changed over time
> > • Include relevant outside information from your knowledge of social studies

In developing your answer to Part III, be sure to keep these explanations in mind:
Identify—means to put a name to or to name.
Define—means to explain features of a thing or concept so that it can be understood.
Argue—means to provide a series of statements that provide evidence and reasons to support a conclusion.

Document 1

AMNESTY INTERNATIONAL

External Document
25 January, 2007

Blood Diamonds are still a reality Conflict or blood diamonds fuel conflict, civil wars and human rights abuses. They have been responsible for funding recent conflicts in Africa which resulted in the death and displacement of millions of people. During these conflicts, profits from the illegal trade in diamonds, worth billions of dollars, were used by warlords and rebels to buy arms. An estimated 3.7 million people have died in Angola, the Democratic Republic of Congo (DRC), Liberia, and Sierra Leone in conflicts fueled by diamonds

While the wars in Angola and Sierra Leone are now over and fighting in the DRC has decreased, the problem of conflict diamonds hasn't gone away.

Despite the fact that an international diamond certification scheme called the Kimberley Process Certification Scheme was launched in 2003, conflict diamonds from Côte d'Ivoire are finding their way through Ghana into the legitimate diamond market. As the brutal conflict in Sierra Leone has shown, even a small amount of conflict diamonds can wreak enormous havoc in a country. Between 1991 and 2002 over 50,000 people were killed, over 2 million displaced within the country or made refugees, and thousands mutilated, raped and tortured. Today, the country is still recovering from the consequences of the conflict.

Document 2

Rain forests play an important role on our planet. By absorbing carbon dioxide and releasing the oxygen that we depend on for our survival. The absorption of this CO2 also helps to stabilize the Earth's climate.

Rainforests also help to maintain the world's water cycle by adding water to the atmosphere through the process of transpiration which creates clouds. Water generated in rainforests travel around the world.

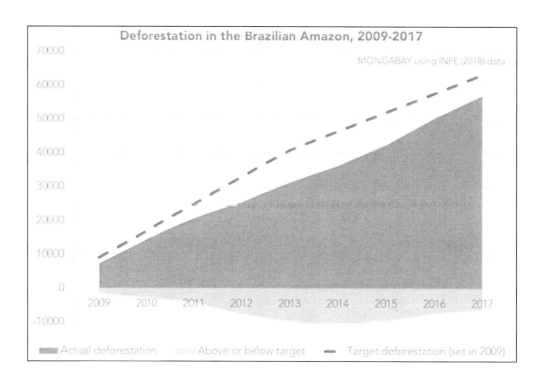

Deforestation in the Brazilian Amazon, 2009-2017

Document 3

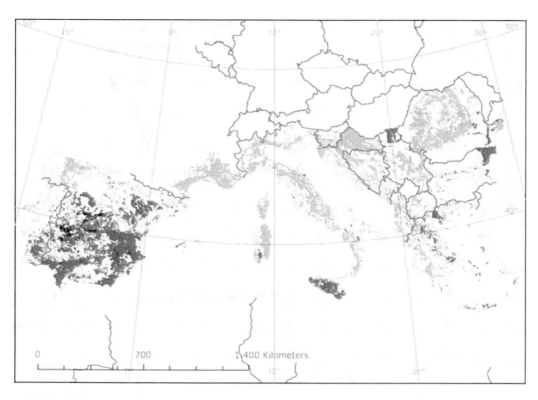

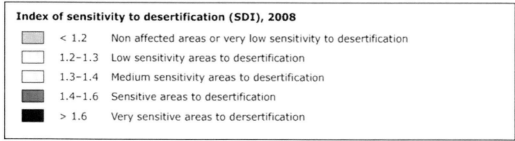

Index of sensitivity to desertification (SDI), 2008

	< 1.2	Non affected areas or very low sensitivity to desertification
	1.2–1.3	Low sensitivity areas to desertification
	1.3–1.4	Medium sensitivity areas to desertification
	1.4–1.6	Sensitive areas to desertification
	> 1.6	Very sensitive areas to dersertification

Document 4

The Register-Mail

96th Year—No. 181 ● Thursday, Aug. 2, 1990 ● Galesburg, Ill. ● 35 Cents

Iraq invades Kuwait over oil

U.S. responds with sanctions; U.N. Council condemns action

KUWAIT (AP) — Iraq's powerful army invaded this small oil-rich kingdom early today. Tank-led troops quickly seized the ruler's palace and government buildings, and the emir fled to Saudi Arabia. Kuwaiti officials said.

The troops have occupied all of Kuwait, one government official shouted down the telephone. Urgent appeals for blood indicated a significant casualty count, but no numbers could be confirmed.

The Revolutionary Command Council led by Iraqi President Saddam Hussein claimed it invaded at the request of revolutionaries who had already overthrown the government and established "The Interim Government of Free Kuwait." Kuwait and U.N. diplomats labeled the coup reports a farce.

The assault followed two weeks of tension between Kuwait and Iraq, caused by Iraqi accusations that Kuwait stole oil from its territory. Saddam also accused Kuwait of exceeding OPEC production quotas, thus driving down the price of oil, a major Iraqi revenue source.

In recent days, diplomats said Iraq had massed more than 100,000 troops at the Kuwait-Iraq border. Kuwait's entire armed forces has 20,300 soldiers.

Kuwait's U.S. ambassador Sheikh Saud Nasir al-Sabah, appealed for help from the United States. "We are asking for military assistance in order to survive," he said in Washington.

A Pentagon source said a naval battle group was diverted toward the region.

Also:

□ Oil prices soared in frenzied trading because of fears the invasion would disrupt supplies. The spot price of North Sea Brent Blend, the most widely traded international crude oil, jumped to $23.62 a barrel from Wednesday's close of $20.40.

□ President Bush signed an order freezing control of Iraqi assets in the United States and blocking most Iraqi imports, including oil. Oil accounts for 97 percent of Iraq's exports into the United States.

□ The U.N. Security Council voted 14-0 to denounce the invasion and demanded immediate withdrawal of Iraqi troops.

Bush said the United States, which has six warships in the Persian Gulf, would "take whatever steps necessary" to defend interests there. Asked if this included military force, Bush said "We're not discussing intervention." But he said he would not discuss military options publicly.

It was the first time in modern history an Arab nation had invaded another and taken over its government.

Kuwait's army was no match for Iraq, battle-hardened after eight years of war with Iran. Iraq has emerged as the Arab world's strongest and most militant military power and Saddam has a vast arsenal of chemical and conventional weapons.

The other Persian Gulf states are politically conservative and have long opposed the use of military force to settle disputes among Arab states.

Diplomats said about 350 Iraqi tanks wheeled into the capital a few hours after crossing the border 40 miles away at dawn. Witnesses said the bombardment of ports and military airports by artillery and the air force was intense.

The invaders surrounded the palace of Kuwait's ruler, Sheik Jaber al-Ahmed al-Sabah, the government of Kuwait said, and area residents said Baghdad said the palace was seized after about two hours of heavy artillery barrages.

There were about 50 tanks around the emir's palace and the neighboring American Embassy, they said.

The Al-Sabah family family has ruled the city-state for almost 250 years. Diplomatic sources in neighboring Saudi Arabia said the emir and the crown prince and prime minister, Sheik Saad al-Abdullah al-Sabah, flew there today.

The Iraqi forces were led by the elite Republican Guard, which did the brunt of fighting in the Iran-Iraq war. Troops set up roadblocks at major intersections and shot at cars that did not stop.

Baghdad television issued communiques it said were from an interim government. One communique said the new government was in "full control of Kuwait City." Others said Kuwait's land and sea borders were closed. They also asked Iraq to maintain security.

The air space over Kuwait was closed.

The television statement said Iraq would withdraw its forces within days or weeks depending on how fast the situation stabilized.

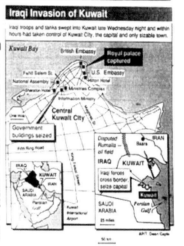

On August 2, 1990, at about 2 a.m. local time, Iraqi forces invade Kuwait, Iraq's tiny, oil-rich neighbor.

Document 5

Napoleon's Invasion of Russia 1812

Napoleon's 600,000 strong Grande Armee cut a three-hundred-mile-wide, six-hundred-mile-deep gash into Russia, always seeking battle. But Russia's smaller, weaker army did not accommodate; it retreated deeper and deeper into the bleak Russian vastness. Even when Russian troops lost pitched battles – notable at Borodino near Moscow, when Russian forces actually performed well – Alexander refused either to throw his entire force into combat or to sue for peace. To Napoleon's disappointment upon entering Moscow, Russian forces and much of the population had left; and to Napoleon's shock, Alexander refused negotiations. Napoleon's prolonged occupation of the Russian capital was fruitless if not pointless, left him with little time before the cold set in, and necessitated what would be a long, disastrous retreat. He admitted in exile that he should have left Moscow far sooner than he did, though that would not have saved the army.

Gompert, David C., et al. "Napoleon's Invasion of Russia, 1812." Blinders, Blunders, and Wars: What America and China Can Learn, RAND Corporation, 2014, pp. 41–52, http://www.jstor.org/stable/10.7249/j.ctt1287m9t.10.

ENDURING ISSUES ESSAY #2

This question is based on the accompanying documents. The question is designed to test your ability to work with historical documents. Some of these documents have been edited for the purposes of this question. As you analyze the documents, take into account the source of each document and any point of view that may be presented in the document. Keep in mind that the language and images used in a document may reflect the historical context of the time in which it was created.

Directions: Read and analyze each of the five documents and write a well-organized essay that includes an introduction, several paragraphs, and a conclusion. Support your response with relevant facts, examples, and details based on your knowledge of social studies and evidence from the documents.

An enduring issue is a challenge or problem that has been debated or discussed across time. An enduring issue is one that many societies have attempted to address with varying degrees of success.

Task:

> • Identify **and** define an enduring issue raised by this set of documents
> • Argue why the issue you selected is significant **and** how it has endured across time
> **In your essay, be sure to**
>   • Identify the enduring issue based on a historically accurate interpretation of at least three documents
>   • Define the issue using relevant evidence from at least three documents
>   • Argue that this is a significant issue that has endured by showing: – How the issue has affected people or has been affected by people – How the issue has continued to be an issue or has changed over time
>   • Include relevant outside information from your knowledge of social studies

In developing your answer to Part III, be sure to keep these explanations in mind:
Identify—means to put a name to or to name.
Define—means to explain features of a thing or concept so that it can be understood.
Argue—means to provide a series of statements that provide evidence and reasons to support a conclusion.

Document 1

In every government there are three sorts of power: the legislative; the executive in respect to things dependent on the law of nations; and the executive in regard to matters that depend on the civil law.

By virtue of the first, the prince or magistrate enacts temporary or perpetual laws, and amends or abrogates those that have been already enacted. By the second, he makes peace or war, sends or receives embassies, establishes the public security, and provides against invasions. By the third, he punishes criminals, or determines the disputes that arise between individuals. The latter we shall call the judiciary power, and the other, simply, the executive power of the state.

When the legislative and executive powers are united in the same person, or in the same body of magistrates, there can be no liberty; because apprehensions may arise, lest the same monarch or senate should enact tyrannical laws, to execute them in a tyrannical manner.

Again, there is no liberty if the judiciary power be not separated from the legislative and executive. Were it joined with the legislative, the life and liberty of the subject would be exposed to arbitrary control; for the judge would be then the legislator. Were it joined to the executive power, the judge might behave with violence and oppression.

There would be an end of every thing, were the same man, or the same body, whether of the nobles or of the people, to exercise those three powers, that of enacting laws, that of executing the public resolutions, and of trying the causes of individuals.

The executive power ought to be in the hands of a monarch, because this branch of government, having need of dispatch, is better administered by one than by many: on the other hand, whatever depends on the legislative power, is oftentimes better regulated by many than by a single person.

But, if there were no monarch, and the executive power should be committed to a certain number of persons, selected from the legislative body, there would be an end of liberty, by reason the two powers would be united; as the same persons would sometimes possess, and would be always able to possess, a share in both.

Montesquieu, De l'Esprit des Lois (1748), Book XI, Chapter 6.[1]

Document 2

Declaration of Human Rights, United Nations (Excerpt)

Article 1
All human beings are born free and equal in dignity and rights. They are endowed with reason and conscience and should act towards one another in a spirit of brotherhood.

Article 2
Everyone is entitled to all the rights and freedoms set forth in this Declaration, without distinction of any kind, such as race, colour, sex, language, religion, political or other opinion, national or social origin, property, birth or other status. Furthermore, no distinction shall be made on the basis of the political, jurisdictional or international status of the country or territory to which a person belongs, whether it be independent, trust, non-self-governing or under any other limitation of sovereignty.

Article 3
Everyone has the right to life, liberty and security of person.

Article 4
No one shall be held in slavery or servitude; slavery and the slave trade shall be prohibited in all their forms.

Article 5
No one shall be subjected to torture or to cruel, inhuman or degrading treatment or punishment.

Document 3

中国人民解放军是毛泽东思想大学校

Cultural Revolution propaganda poster. It depicts Mao Zedong, above
a group of soldiers from the People's Liberation Army. The caption
reads, "The Chinese People's Liberation Army is the great school of
Mao Zedong Thought."

Document 4

Karl Marx's "10 Planks" of the *Communist Manifesto:*

1. Abolition of Property in Land and Application of all Rents of Land to Public Purpose.

2. A Heavy Progressive or Graduated Income Tax.

3. Abolition of All Rights of Inheritance.

4. Confiscation of the Property of All Emigrants and Rebels.

5. Centralization of Credit in the Hands of the State, by Means of a National Bank with State Capital and an Exclusive Monopoly.

6. Centralization of the Means of Communication and Transport in the Hands of the State.

7. Extension of Factories and Instruments of Production Owned by the State, the Bringing Into Cultivation of Waste Lands, and the Improvement of the Soil Generally in Accordance with a Common Plan.

8. Equal Liability of All to Labor. Establishment of Industrial Armies, Especially for Agriculture.

9. Combination of Agriculture with Manufacturing Industries; Gradual Abolition of the Distinction Between Town and Country by a More Equable Distribution of the Population over the Country.

10. Free Education for All Children in Public Schools. Abolition of Children's Factory Labor in it's Present Form. Combination of Education with Industrial Production.

Document 5

The White Man's Burden: Rudyard Kipling

Take up the White Man's burden—
Send forth the best ye breed—
Go send your sons to exile
To serve your captives' need
To wait in heavy harness
On fluttered folk and wild—
Your new-caught, sullen peoples,
Half devil and half child
Take up the White Man's burden
In patience to abide
To veil the threat of terror
And check the show of pride;
By open speech and simple
A hundred times made plain
To seek another's profit
And work another's gain

ANSWERS

Scientific Revolution

1. 3
2. 1
3. 4
4. 1
5. 4
6. 2
7. 3
8. 1
9. 4
10. 3

Enlightenment Era

1. 3
2. 1
3. 2
4. 4
5. 1
6. 2
7. 3
8. 2
9. 1
10. 4

French Revolution

1. 2
2. 3
3. 1
4. 3
5. 4
6. 1
7. 2
8. 2
9. 4
10. 3

Nationalism

1. 2
2. 3
3. 4
4. 3
5. 3
6. 2
7. 4
8. 2
9. 1
10. 4

Industrial Revolution

1. 2
2. 1
3. 3
4. 3
5. 1
6. 4
7. 3
8. 3
9. 1
10. 2

Imperialism

1. 2
2. 4
3. 1
4. 3
5. 3
6. 4
7. 1
8. 3
9. 2
10. 1

ANSWERS

World War 1
1. 2
2. 1
3. 3
4. 1
5. 4
6. 1
7. 3
8. 1
9. 4
10. 2

World War 2
1. 3
2. 2
3. 1
4. 3
5. 4
6. 2
7. 1
8. 3
9. 2
10. 4

Russian Revolution
1. 3
2. 1
3. 3
4. 4
5. 1
6. 3
7. 2
8. 1
9. 3
10. 2

Cold War
1. 2
2. 4
3. 3
4. 1
5. 4
6. 1
7. 2
8. 3
9. 4
10. 2

Inter-War Years
1. 2
2. 3
3. 1
4. 3
5. 1
6. 4
7. 1
8. 3
9. 1
10. 2

Chinese Revolution
1. 4
2. 1
3. 3
4. 2
5. 4
6. 1
7. 3
8. 4
9. 1
10. 3

ANSWERS

Decolonization
1. 2
2. 4
3. 1
4. 3
5. 1
6. 3
7. 4
8. 1
9. 2
10. 1

International Hot Spots
1. 3
2. 4
3. 1
4. 1
5. 2
6. 1
7. 3
8. 4
9. 2
10. 3

The Middle East
1. 2
2. 3
3. 1
4. 3
5. 1
6. 4
7. 3
8. 1
9. 4
10. 2

Human Rights Violations
1. 3
2. 2
3. 1
4. 1
5. 4
6. 2
7. 1
8. 2
9. 4
10. 2

Latin America
1. 2
2. 1
3. 4
4. 1
5. 3
6. 2
7. 3
8. 1
9. 3
10. 2

The World Today
1. 2
2. 4
3. 4
4. 1
5. 2
6. 1
7. 1
8. 2
9. 4
10. 3

WORD PUZZLE REVIEW

Name _____ Date _____

IMPERIALISM

```
E A Y R E R K S U F P D G X M W S E
N A B C H E Q I V P P K B J H L C W
O O S N I Q B Z N I U O Y I J N J Y
I P S T R L C P N G E W T A E L C B
L I L T I K O M F R L E N U M I S E
L U Q B F N T P W U M E L S L Y R R
E M Y M B Y D A R A X F O O R K E L
B W M Y C U R I N O N J P P F T O I
E A T G R K A S A I O N W W O V B N
R R U P M T B E F C G D Y N O L O C
R S J O K U R O R I O N N H E X D O
E Y B C R X S A E R R M X E A A U N
X L A D K E R R V Y R E P R P T J F
O A E S R C O C Q W B I V A P O A E
B N J E E F L C M D Y O J Y N Q R R
W G H I M P E R I A L I S M J Y P E
Y P M S I N I W R A D L A I C O S N
S C R A M B L E F O R A F R I C A C
O Y U Y I X K U U P Y E A U Q G O E
Y F S X Z D W Q L Z C O E N C X O G
M D V W O M K L C I U U P S R N Q I
L J Y E Z U P Q W S G R X E I O N I
L L J J V X L B A R L G D P S B S G
```

Word Bank
BERLIN CONFERENCE
BOERS
BOER WAR
BOXER REBELLION
COLONY
FAST INDIA COMPANY
FOREIGN POLICY
IMPERIALISM
OPEN DOOR POLICY
OPIUM WARS
SCRAMBLE FOR AFRICA
SEPOY
SOCIAL DARWINISM
SPHERES OF INFLUENCE
WHITE MANS BURDEN

Use the clues and the word bank to fill in the terms. The first letter has been provided.

W _____ -- Poem: duty of whites to control non-whites for their own good
S _____ -- Belief that only strongest countries will survive & control others
I _____ -- Extending power & influence through diplomacy or military force
F _____ -- Nation's overall plan for dealing with other nations
O _____ -- U.S. policy for equal trade privileges for all countries with China
B _____ -- Anti-imperialism uprising in China
S _____ -- Area of economic and political control without direct rule
E _____ -- British company formed for trade with Asia and India
S _____ -- Indian soldier
O _____ -- European wars with China to defend the opium trade
B _____ -- Dutch, French and German settlers of South Africa
B _____ -- War between Great Britain and Boers in South Africa
S _____ -- Invasion, occupation and division of Africa by European powers
B _____ -- Negotiated European colonization and trade in Africa
C _____ -- An area controlled by a foreign government

IMPERIALISM

```
E A Y R E R K S U F P D G X M W S E
N A B C H E Q I V P P K B J H L C W
O O S N I Q B Z N I U O Y I J N J Y
I P S T R L C P N G E W T A E L C B
L I L T I K O M F R L E N U M I S E
L U Q B F N T P W U M E L S L Y R R
E M Y M B Y D A R A X F O O R K E L
B W M Y C U R I N O N J P P F T O I
E A T G R K A S A I O N W W O V B N
R R U P M T B E F C G D Y N O L O C
R S J O K U R O R I O N N H E X D O
E Y B C R X S A E R R M X E A A U N
X L A D K E R R V Y R E P R P T J F
O A E S R C O C Q W B I V A P O A E
B N J E E F L C M D Y O J Y N Q R R
W G H I M P E R I A L I S M J Y P E
Y P M S I N I W R A D L A I C O S N
S C R A M B L E F O R A F R I C A C
O Y U Y I X K U U P Y E A U Q G O E
Y F S X Z D W Q L Z C O E N C X O G
M D V W O M K L C I U U P S R N Q I
L J Y E Z U P Q W S G R X E I O N I
L L J J V X L B A R L G D P S B S G
```

Use the clues and the word bank to fill in the terms. The first letter has been provided.

White Man's Burden -- Alleged duty of whites to control non-whites for their own good
Social Darwinism -- Belief that only strongest countries will survive and control others
Imperialism -- Extending power and influence through diplomacy or military force
Foreign Policy -- Nation's overall plan for dealing with other nations
Open Door Policy -- U.S. policy for equal trade privileges for all countries with China
Boxer Rebellion -- Anti-imperialism uprising in China
Spheres of Influence -- Area of economic and political control without direct rule
East India Company -- British company formed for trade with Asia and India
Sepoy -- Indian soldier
Opium Wars -- European wars with China to defend the opium trade
Boers -- Dutch, French and German settlers of South Africa
Boer War -- War between Great Britain and Boers in South Africa
Scramble for Africa -- Invasion, occupation and division of Africa by European powers
Berlin Conference -- Negotiated European colonization and trade in Africa
King Leopold -- Belgian king that founded the Congo Free State in Africa
Colony -- An area controlled by a foreign government

WORLD WAR I

```
T D K L H R Q R B A Z X M C R V A I
T R B Q W E S T E R N F R O N T B M
R S E V V D Q N M C X U E P S A G P
I T S A F W O C R H L F E M T G E E
H Q J Z T R X O J D W G A T R M R R
Z R P Y A Y W Q J U Z T L Z I G A I
N R Q B H S O K B K N E W L U N F A
R X D H G R M F B E O Z I Y S P R L
S E R A N E M Q V F R T W R Q B A I
R R R N P A D B T E A S D K X R W S
D V E T S D T H J R R V U X Y S H M
S N L W F D E I I D F S E L R H C G
E L A P O S E S O I V Q A E W I N T
C O Z H O P M M Z N F J W I P H E S
N A P M K S L K C A A O D C L L R K
A S M T N C N A A N P L N P O L T K
I E A U B O A T R D H Y I V F K E U
L Y D K Z G W L E T M D W S X U D S
L I P X Q N W I B K N D G L M Z Y N
A U N Q Q Y L Q T E C E I O F Q Y J
D K D N A L S N A M O N C L R E J Q
D T C G A D R B O B S R R T L A D D
I I S A L O H C I N R A S T K L L X
```

Use the clues and the word bank to fill in the terms. The first letter has been provided.

Archduke Ferdinand -- His assassination launched WWI
Black Hand -- Secret society behind assassination of Archduke Ferdinand
Nationalism - Extreme pride in one's country
Militarism - A nation prioritizes military build-up
Imperialism - When a strong nation controls a weaker one
Alliances - 2 or more nations agree to protect each other
Allied Powers -- WWI alliance between Britain, France, Russia Italy, and Japan
Central Powers -- WWI alliance between Germany and others vs. Allied Powers
Red Baron -- German fighter pilot
No Man's Land -- The area between the front lines of two enemy armies
Trench warfare -- Defensively each side digs lines of trenches for protection
U Boat -- A German submarine
Western Front-- A region of fighting between France and Germany
Battle of the Somme -- Major WWI battle fought near the Somme River
Nicholas II -- Last Russian czar , withdrew Russia from WWI
Treaty of Versailles -- Peace treaty that ended World War I

COLD WAR

T	S	P	D	T	G	E	Y	W	R	N	O	S	J	X	A	X	D
U	M	V	R	D	R	S	S	E	C	O	M	N	Y	O	T	V	W
T	K	A	M	O	A	J	W	W	D	I	O	T	R	A	C	H	K
L	C	O	R	A	X	O	F	E	F	T	Y	E	G	E	O	U	K
S	L	A	V	S	P	Y	T	F	S	A	C	H	N	T	L	U	Z
P	I	I	P	R	H	E	W	U	D	N	U	I	Y	J	D	F	G
S	D	S	E	W	N	A	Y	A	F	E	R	T	N	Q	W	W	P
Q	K	P	I	T	A	K	L	V	R	T	T	C	K	S	A	Q	A
L	U	O	E	R	J	S	J	L	C	I	C	U	J	K	R	Y	R
S	T	N	B	B	C	Q	R	O	P	L	V	P	P	C	Q	R	V
C	S	P	A	U	D	E	D	A	E	L	W	X	C	J	M	L	V
I	D	Y	F	E	T	N	L	R	W	E	A	N	W	F	Z	L	K
M	V	V	D	V	A	I	K	I	K	T	O	N	I	H	Z	A	C
P	Y	X	Y	M	G	R	P	G	S	A	G	D	R	S	G	W	M
K	H	K	U	M	C	O	F	R	T	S	E	I	T	W	E	N	N
G	J	R	U	L	H	N	D	D	S	L	I	V	W	L	Q	I	S
K	T	K	H	O	P	C	X	V	C	R	A	M	L	D	K	L	J
F	N	L	W	Y	X	U	X	A	Y	S	C	C	N	C	B	R	M
X	J	N	P	G	M	R	S	C	A	R	M	S	R	A	C	E	M
D	O	M	I	N	O	T	H	E	O	R	Y	X	S	F	B	B	Y
K	V	X	Y	O	R	A	O	T	A	N	I	C	Q	P	S	U	K
M	I	M	W	O	G	I	T	N	E	M	N	I	A	T	N	O	C
T	U	D	B	T	W	N	Y	U	H	I	Q	L	G	A	E	I	N

Word Bank

ARMS RACE
BERLIN WALL
COLD WAR
CONTAINMENT
CUBAN MISSILE CRISIS
DETENTE
DOMINO THEORY
FIDEL CASTRO
IRON CURTAIN
MARSHALL PLAN
NATO
PROXY WAR
SATELLITE NATION
SUPERPOWER
TRUMAN DOCTRINE
WARSAW PACT

Use the clues and the word bank to fill in the terms. The first letter has been provided.

C _____ -- Post-World War II world-wide conflict over communism
A _____ -- Competition for military supremacy
D _____ -- U.S. belief that if 1 nation fell to communism many would follow
M _____ -- U.S. financial aid to European countries
T _____ -- Economic Aid to Turkey & Greece
W _____ -- Soviet Union & Eastern European countries defense alliance
N _____ -- Western European defense coalition (initials)
I _____ -- Symbolic border between communist and non-communist Europe
B _____ -- Border built to separate East and West Berlin
F _____ -- Cuban revolutionary that set up a communist state in Cuba
S _____ -- Nation dominated by another politically and economically
P _____ -- Use of third parties instead of fighting each other directly
S _____ -- Post WWII the Soviets and U.S. each became a world _____
D _____ -- Effort to reduce tension between superpowers
C _____ -- Keeping something (such as communism) at the current status
C _____ -- Soviet missiles in Cuba brought U.S. to brink of war

MRBM LAUNCH SITE 2
SAN CRISTOBAL
1 NOVEMBER 1962

COLD WAR

Answer Key

```
C A P K S O X L H C T G Y T I S H E
U U D E S G N C O N Z R R Z X A W R
V L B B R Z I M G R E U F U M T A A
S B F A L E M P L I M G C G S E R C
U U T V N U S Z F A Q C I C U L S S
L F D Z N M E T N O M B F T D L A D
Z W Q I F X I D R Y Y J G H O I W E
G U S N R U O S L O V A G X X T P R
D M H Y L C V P S F I L B T J E A R
I Q F V T T U P P I C K A B M N C N
D C M R R M F K S X L J A S M A T A
N S I H S Z L I O J C E I D M T R L
H N P P I P G B L M X Y C B K I E P
E W T U A M S X K R H X A R E O S L
S N O I T A N D E T I N U C I N M L
S A R A W N A E R O K A A P Y S Y A
Y T I X J S I A B S U R N A S G I H
T O L P G H C K T C S T A I Y U J S
L F L B O C L F T M S L A Y L P Z R
J L P N M F T M R T E G C X B R Y A
M Q K H F G L A S N O S T A Q M E M
I R O N C U R T A I N A U F Q M V B
W O I A Q O M D Q T X H E F G G M V
```

United Nations -- International body of nations to settle disputes and world problems
Marshall Plan -- European relief plan to assist post-WWII reconstruction
Communism -- Theory in which collective ownership leads to a classless society
NATO -- North Atlantic Treaty Organization; anti-Soviet bloc of nations
Warsaw Pact -- Alliance of European communist nations
Truman Doctrine -- Truman foreign policy pledging to resist communism
Satellite nations -- Communist nations in Eastern Europe under USSR influence
McCarthyism -- Often unjust attempt to root out communists from various institutions
Red Scare -- Fear of communist infiltration of U.S.
Berlin Airlift -- Means to deliver supplies to West Berlin during USSR blockade
Iron Curtain -- Metaphor for boundary of communist controlled areas of Europe
Korean War -- Civil war in Korea that became post-WWII anti-communist U.S. conflict
Arms Race -- Military contest between U.S. and USSR for supremacy
Sputnik -- First man-made satellite to orbit Earth launched by Soviet Union
Bay of Pigs -- U.S. supported attempt to overturn Fidel Castro
Cuban Missile Crisis -- International incident arising from Soviet missile base in Cuba
Glasnost - "Openness" in the Soviet Union to reform
Perestroika -- "Restructuring" in the Soviet Union; economic and social reforms

Glossary

A

African National Congress (AFC): Organization formed in opposition to Apartheid in S. Africa

AIDS: Acquired immune deficiency syndrome, a disease lowering the body's immune system

Allied Powers: World War 1 and World War 2 alliance between nations opposed to the Central Powers (WW1) and Axis Powers (WW2)

anti-Semitism: prejudice against Jews

Apartheid: Policy of segregation in S. Africa

appeasement: policy of giving into an aggressor's demand to avoid conflict

B

Berlin Conference: 1884 meeting of European nations with the aim of dividing Africa among themselves

Bloody Sunday: Russian workers protested and were fired on by soldiers

Boer War: Between the British and Dutch farmers (Boers) from 1899-1902 caused by Britain attempted annexation of the Boer republics in Africa

Bolshevik: Russian communist revolutionary group

Boxer Rebellion: Chinese uprising against foreigners

C

capitalism: an economic system where individuals own the means of production

Central Powers: World War 1 alliance of Germany, Austria-Hungary and the Ottomans, later Bulgaria

civil disobedience: the act of disobeying an unjust law

Cold War: period of tension and hostility between the United States and Soviet Union (1945-1990)

collective: large farms run by a group of people (Soviet Union and China)

Command economy: economic system where the state controls the means of production

Committee of Public Safety: political body during the French Revolution

concentration camp: detainment facilities run by Germany during World War 2 imprisoning mainly Jews

Congress of Vienna: 1815 meeting held in Europe with the goal of restoring order after Napoleon's reign

containment: United States policy during the Cold War trying to stop the spread of communism

Contras: a counterrevolutionary group in Nicaragua supported by the United States.

Coup d'état: a group of rebels attempting to overthrow a government

Cultural Revolution: A movement in China led by Mao Zedong in 1966 attempting to reinvigorate his ideologies and purge opponents

czar: an absolute leader in Russia (also tsar)

D

Declaration of the Rights of Man: document written during the French Revolution inspired by the Declaration of Independence

decolonization: the process of granting independence to former European colonies

deforestation: the mass removal of forests, especially rain forests

desertification: spreading of deserts due to over farming and draught

détente: lessening of tensions between the United States and Soviet Union during the Cold War

Developing nation: a country that is industrializing slowly

Dirty War: a period in Argentina (1970s) when the government detained and killed perceived opponents

Domino Theory: the belief that if 1 nation fell to communism many more would follow.

Duma: legislative body in Russia

E

Encomienda: a Spanish system of governing in the Americas that allowed landowners to demand labor from the indigenous people

Enlightenment: an Era beginning in Europe when people questioned traditional ideas and types of government

Estate General: a legislative body in France consisting of clergy, nobles and commoners

ethnic cleansing: killing or removing an ethnic group

ethnocentrism: the belief that one ethnicity is superior to others

euro: currency created with the advent of the European Union

European Union: An alliance of European countries beginning in the 1980s

F

Fascism: a type of government run by a dictator that is imperialistic and nationalistic

feudalism: a system where land is given to nobles in exchange for protection

five-year plan: an attempt to quickly industrialize and increase farm output implemented by Joseph Stalin in the Soviet Union

G

Genocide: attempt to destroy an ethnic or religious group

Glasnost: a policy of openness instituted by Mikhail Gorbachev in the Soviet Union

Great Depression: worldwide economic downturn

Great Leap Forward: an attempt to industrialize and increase farm output implemented by Mao Zedong in China

Green Revolution: big changes in farming methods that resulted in higher output

Greenhouse effect: rising temperatures caused by the increase of carbon dioxide in the atmosphere

H

Holocaust: name given to the genocide of Jews by the Nazis during World War 2

Holy Land: area in Palestine that is holy to Jews, Muslims and Christians

I

Imperialism: when a strong nation controls a weaker politically, economically and/or socially

Indian National Congress: Organization created to gain Indian independence

Indigenous: native to an area

Industrial Revolution: change in how goods are produced, in factories rather than by hand, began in Britain

International Monetary Fund (IMF): Group that mediated for debtors nations beginning in the 1980s

Intifada: Palestinian uprising against Jewish rule in Israel

Iron curtain: imaginary line dividing Soviet satellite nations in eastern Europe and western democratic nations

Islamic fundamentalism:: Muslim movement against westernization led by reformers who want Islamic principles in their countries

J

Jacobins: radical political group during the French Revolution

L

laissez faire: economic policy whereby government does not interfere with business

League of Nations: Organization formed after World War 1 to promote peace

Long March: retreat by the communists during China's civil war, led by Mao Zedong

M

Marshall Plan: United States gave economic aid to western Europe to rebuild after World War 2

Meiji Restoration: a period of rapid modernization in Japan (1868-1912)

Militarism: prioritizing military buildup

Mosque: place of worship for Muslims

Munich Agreement: 1938 agreement to allow Germany to control the Sudetenland

Muslim League: organization formed in India to advocate for the rights of Muslims during its independence movement

N

National Assembly: group formed in 1789 by the third Estate to institute democratic changes in France

Nationalism: a feeling of pride in one's country

NATO: North Atlantic Treaty Organization: an alliance of western nations formed during the Cold War and still active today

Natural rights: the idea that all individual have basic rights that cannot be taken away

No mans land: area between opposing trenches

O

OPEC: Organization of Petroleum Exporting Countries formed to set oil prices

Opium Wars: 1839 conflict between Britain and China over opium trade

ozone layer: layer of gases high in the atmosphere that are being depleted

P

Palestinian Liberation Organization (PLO): organization created to form a Palestinian nation

Pan-Africanism: a movement to unite African countries

Pan-Arabism: a movement to unite Arabic peoples

Perestroika: capitalistic policies instituted in the Soviet Union in the 1980s

Persian Gulf War: In 1991 a group of countries sent troops to Kuwait to drive out the invading nation of Iraq

pogroms: violent attacks against Jews in Russia

purge: eliminating a group of people from a country

Q

Quran: holy book of Islam

R

republic: a political system where citizens elect representatives

Russification: A movement by Russian rulers to force all ethnic groups to adopt Russian culture

Russo-Japanese War: Conflict in 1904 between Russia and Japan ending in Japanese victory

S

Sandinistas: revolutionary group that took power in Nicaragua in 1979

Satellite: eastern European nations under Soviet influence during the Cold War

Secular: separating religion from government

Sepoy Mutiny: rebellion by sepoy Indian soldiers against British rule

Sharia: Islamic laws

Shiite: a main sect of Islam

Soviet: a group of workers set up by revolutionaries in Russia

Sphere of influence: having economic control over part of a country

Sunni: a main sect of Islam

T

Taiping Rebellion: Chinese uprising against foreign interference

tariff: a tax on imported goods

terrorism: violence, including against civilians for political purposes

Trade deficit: a nation that imports more goods than it exports

Treaty of Kanagawa: Agreement to allow the United States to trade in Japan

Treaty of Nanjing: Treaty at the end of the Opium war between Britain and China

Trench warfare: fighting in long ditches

Truman Doctrine: economic aid to help nations resist Soviet influence

U

United Nations: organization created after World War 2 to maintain world peace and support economic growth of nations

Universal Declaration of Human Rights: document created by the United Nations listing rights for all people

Urbanization: rapid growth of cities

W

Warsaw Pact: military alliance between the Soviet Union and its satellites

westernization: adopting western (European and American) culture

Z

Zionism: Jews' desire for a homeland

Made in United States
North Haven, CT
16 May 2023

36632029R10078